Don't Make Me Pull Over!

by
Lori Clinch

... voted favorite columnist of the year
for both 2004 and 2005

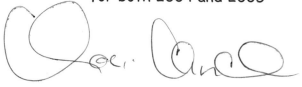

The Old Hundred and One Press
North Platte, Nebraska 69101

Copyright © 2006 by Lori Clinch

All rights reserved. No part of this book may be reproduced or utilized in any form or by any means, electronic or mechanical, including photocopying, recording, or by any information storage and retrieval system, without permission in writing from the Publisher.

Published by
The Old Hundred and One Press
2220 Leota
North Platte, Nebraska 69101

Printed in the United States of America
by
The Covington Group
Kansas City, Missouri
Cover Design by
Diane J. Solomon
Seattle, Washington
Illustrations by Lori Allberry
Interior Book Design by
Robin Waters - Graphic Arts Unlimited
North Platte, Nebraska
Edited by Theresa McGahan

Library of Congress number: 2006926235

Don't Make Me Pull Over! by Lori Clinch
p. cm
ISBN 0-976367645

"Just when I thought I was the only one with a plugged up stool, screaming kids and a husband who comes home and asks, 'What did you do all day?' It's comforting to know that I'm not alone."
—Trixie

"*Don't Make Me Pull Over!* is the ultimate field guide for all mothers, mothers-to-be, and empty-nesting friends of mothers. It's replete with EUREKA moments of discovering a kindred spirit who validates those mom feelings from where you are, what you want to be, or been there, done that and I prefer hindsight! Lori captures the schizophrenia parenting rollercoaster of 'I adore my kids but for 2 cents I'd give them away if I could find anyone crazy enough to take them.' "It's all about HER—but it's also all about US. As her friend and confidante, even I would never act up and tempt her to pull over...she'd do it! ...then she'd come back and get me."
—The Empty Nesting Eunice

"Of all of the people that I have ever met, Lori is one of them."
—Ethel

"*Don't Make Me Pull Over!* will instantly place a smile on every mother's face. Lori takes everyday life experiences and creates very visual and entertaining stories for us to take pleasure in. She sees the humor in her day to day family activities and draws us in by the wit and wisdom of her writings. Her Erma Bombeck take on life allows her the opportunity to keep life light-hearted and full of laughter. Her clever writing sets the stage and we feel as though we are in the front row of her family's production. We can't wait for the second act! You will want Lori to pull over so you can introduce yourself to the person that changed your outlook on raising kids and having a family"
—Karen O'Connor

"Lori Clinch's columns are so good that I'm tempted to tell people I wrote them myself. Problem is, people would never believe I'm married to some guy named Pat."
—Dave Simpson, editor,
The North Platte Telegraph

"Raising kids can be a humiliating experience. By weaving humor, with the antics of her brood, Lori Clinch makes the lessons learned, more palatable for herself and the reader! Lori has a unique manner of melding hip-youth-lingo, current events, and her own inadequacies into captivating tales that will either bring the reader an outright burst of laughter, a smile, or a mental "been there, done that!" (Incidentally, she paid me to say the good stuff ☺)"
—Pat Jones
Lori's favorite cousin!!!

"I laughed a great deal when I read Lori Clinch's stories about how to deal with CRS (Can't Remember Stuff). I just wish I could remember what she said."
—Mabel

"I've been a big fan of Lori Clinch ever since she first sent me her column and challenged me to a humor duel. After losing gracefully—I'm nothing if not a gentleman—I've become a regular reader and stealer of her ideas. I'm especially happy to see that she has compiled them into a simple, easy-to-plagiarize book form, as searching all over the Internet was becoming tiresome. I am proud to recommend this book to anyone with $15.95 in their pocket, or at least the ability to outrun bookstore security."
— Erik Deckers,
Laughing Stalk humor columnist
Laughing Stalk Syndicate
www.humorcolumnists.com

"So many of the things that Lori says to her children she has heard her father and me say at one time or another. With that in mind, I'm sure she realizes the revelation in her Dad's favorite saying: 'What goes around, comes around.'"
—Mom & Dad

"As the father of three sons, I get an eerie feeling of déjà vu whenever I read a column by Lori Clinch. I've been there, I think. She's writing about my life. That's the mark of a great columnist, the ability to cut a little slice from the pie of life that we've all enjoyed, or at least lived through — if that pie was made of under-cooked pumpkin chunks by crazy old Aunt Hazel — and serve it back to us in a more entertaining form.

"Like the great scientist Charles Darwin cataloging new species and behaviors as he traveled uncharted lands, Lori chronicles the ups and downs of family life and parenthood with a fresh and loving eye, sometimes overjoyed, often chagrined by life's bounty and unpredictability. But her observations and pronouncements are always made with good humor and the unspoken understanding that despite the challenges, and sometimes despite the outright frustration that comes with raising a family of demanding sons and a husband who puts her in 'chore boots', there's no place in the world she'd rather be (all right, maybe she'd take a weekend on an island with cool shoes, a good book, and lots of iced fruit drinks with umbrellas, but she couldn't stay away for long). And her columns always bring a smile—an incredibly valuable commodity in today's world.

"In my business, I meet lots of people who think they can be columnists. And many of them even come up with a few good columns before they run out of inspiration, material, and gas. Lori, though, is the real deal. Her work is always fresh and insightful, and usually laugh-out-loud funny. The fact that she seems to be writing about my life — and maybe yours as well — is just icing on the cake."
— *Greg Bean, Executive Editor*
Greater Media Newspapers
Freehold, New Jersey

Acknowledgements

I would like to thank the people who have made this book possible—first of all my husband and children, for if they sat still, treated each other with respect, and didn't react to situations with wit and one-liners, there'd be little to write about. I'd also like to thank my parents, who not only behave more like the Barones than the Cleavers, but who laugh themselves silly when I ask them to watch the kids so my husband and I can leave town for the weekend.

Special thanks to Theresa McGahan, The One Hundred and One Press and especially Billie Thornburg for her faith and confidence in me. She's made my dreams come true.

I'm very grateful to Caryl Simpson, Toni Slattery, Patricia Jones, and Karen O'Connor who edit my stuff before I send it to an editor—they almost make me look like I'm smart.

Speaking of editors, without Dave Simpson, my exposure would still be limited to Christmas letters and emails that start with, "You'll never guess what those kids did today!" Thanks, Dave, for giving me the chance.

I would also like to thank Greater Media Editor, Greg Bean, who often times gives me fodder for my column and insists that my family won't be mentally healthy until I hang a buffalo skull on the wall in the living room.

Dedication

To my husband, Pat, and to my children who are known in my columns as Vernon, Huey, Lawrence, and Little Charlie. I could not ask for more than a family who acts up, acts out, and then lets me write about it.

TABLE OF CONTENTS

1. So Much For Child Rearing Advice 1
2. Golf 4
3. The Purse 7
4. Lunar Calendar Adjustment 10
5. Time To Toss The Drab 13
6. No More Pencils, No More Books 16
7. Warning: This Gal Stops At All Garage Sales 19
8. The Wagoneer 22
9. Curry's Cicadas 25
10. Bending Rebar 28
11. Making The Kids Do Laundry 31
12. Remember Bad Car Trips? 34
13. Turning Forty 37
14. Potty Training 40
15. Telemarketers 43
16. I'm Sorry, Who Are You? 46
17. Mama Tried But Her Boy Loves Country 49
18. Second Thoughts On Back To School 52
19. So Much For Ignoring The Problem 55
20. It's So Easy That I Can't Stinking Believe It! 58
21. Raising Ralphie 61
22. Offsides, On The Offense 64
23. The Dreaded Teenage Party 67
24. In Search Of The Isomer 70
25. Speech For All Seasons:
    There's Nothing To Eat Around Here! 73
26. Housekeeping And The Chaos Theory 76
27. Weigh-In Adds Insult To Injury 79
28. Parenting Advice From Dr. Hasnokids 82
29. When In Doubt, Blame The Reception 85
30. Fabio vs. Bob 88
31. This Hole In The Wall Gang Hangs Pictures 91

32. The Snow Day: Cruel and Unusual 94
33. The Key To Any Teenager's Heart: $5 97
34. What The Towel Did That Kid Just Say? 100
35. He Wants $125 Shoes For Christmas 103
36. He Makes Driving Off Sound Simple 106
37. A Bad Case Of The 'Man Hands' 109
38. Hold That Diet Until The Fudge Is Gone 112
39. Take This Pill And Run With The Puppies 115
40. Another Driver's License Photo Casualty 118
41. Quick Trip Turns Into $257 Shopping Spree 121
42. No Rest For The Weary On Homework 124
43. How Was Your Day? Better Not Ask 127
44. Sometimes A Bad Memory Comes In Handy 130
45. Time To Purge The Holiday Leftovers 133
46. Oh No! Here Comes The Principal! 136
47. Young Cell Phone Fan Stuck At Point D 139
48. But Honey, It's A Small Dump Truck 142
49. Mom's Crabby 'Til Someone Buys The House 145
50. Lawnmowers Should Never Go Thunk 148
51. Moving To The Country 151
52. No Time To Worry About Skin Tone 154
53. So Long Tranquility, Hello Summer 157
54. Svelte Fanny Is So Out Of The Club 160
55. And Now, A Real Moving Experience 163
56. Pasta Collage Goes Way Of All Flesh 166
57. Boredom Descends On Summer Break 169
58. Moving With Pat 172
59. It's Not Insipid, It's The Super Hero Look 175
60. A Perfect Place For Aunt Patti's Gifts 178
61. Drop In Company 181
62. Dropping In On Others 184
63. Triathalons Are Not My Cup Of Sweat 187
64. Nobody, But Nobody Can Move Dirt Like Mother 190
65. Back To School Silence Is Golden 193

66. Keeping Up With Tommy's Mom 196
67. Blah, Blah, Blah, Expensive, Blah, Blah 199
68. So Much For The Boys Protecting Mom 202
69. Kids! If It Isn't One Thing, It's Another 205
70. Falling Short Of Mother Of The Year 208
71. There's More To Life Than An RX7 211
72. Yet Another Darned Bug Collection 214
73. Laurel Alley Irons 217
74. For High-Tech Stuff, You Need A Kid 220
75. Busted Over A Dirty Pair Of Socks 223
76. What Was That Kid's Name Again? 226
77. A Vicious Cycle At The Doctor's Office 229
78. Paprika Makes Up For What Meals Lack 232
79. Possum Remedy Isn't For Faint Of Heart 235
80. No Mistaking Who That Kid Was 238
81. Looking Forward To The Christmas Wee Hours 241
82. How I Scared The Burglar Away 244
83. Flu Bug Comes Home For The Holidays 247
84. Cap'n Tightwad Puts Lid On Spending 250
85. Close Call Puts New Spin On Calls 253
86. Who Could Have Thrown Cookie Away? 256
87. No Tomfoolery And I Mean It! 259
88. Death By Mirrors At The Clothing Store 262
89. Curse Words And Confession 265
90. A New Empty Nester Shows No Mercy 268

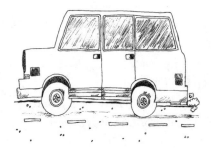

1

SO MUCH FOR CHILD REARING ADVICE

I am a firm believer in the benefits of a good old-fashioned temper tantrum. I wait for the proper predicament to occur, then I clench my fist, set my jaw, and stomp like a raving lunatic.

It would be much more enjoyable if my husband would get irritated enough to join me now and then. Yet, while I'm bouncing my head off of the nearest wall, he stands there and smiles sweetly. As if that weren't bad enough, he then pats me on the back and assures me with, "You're right. You're always right."

"I am NOT right!" I screamed at him the other day. "Don't you stand there and tell me that I'm right. Maybe you're the one who's right. Did you ever think of that?"

He didn't respond. Instead he left me alone to ponder the fact that I may be right and it was making me spittin' mad just to think about it.

Why should he get to be the one with the patience of a saint?

This is especially true where our children are concerned. On a recent car trip, I'd planned to sit in the passenger seat and bide my time. Let the kids get under his skin for once, while I read a magazine and ignored their antics.

About 15 minutes into the car ride, things started to heat up quite nicely. A smack, a poke, and a blood-curdling scream followed a quick jab; it was just as I'd expected.

"Now, now boys," I said calmly at first, not even turning to look, "let's not fight. Commemorate the Golden Rule, stay precious, and remember, Mommy loves." Then I smiled sweetly at my husband who hadn't seemed to notice the confrontation, patted him on the shoulder, and went back to my parenting magazine.

I was engrossed with suggestion number two of an article entitled, "Sharpen Your Disciplinary Skills," when the verbal zingers began to ring out from the back seat.

"You are an idiot!" filled the air and was quickly followed by, "Yeah, well you are a moron!"

"Let's refrain from obscenities," I said, speaking in a hushed tone as suggestion number two of the disciplinary article suggested. If my beloved spouse could be patient and ignore this outburst, then so could I.

When the fighting escalated, I turned to face the little dears and said, "Let's keep to ourselves children and do our best to maintain composure. Anyone up for a rousing game of license plate bingo?"

I got no takers. However, little Huey saw it as an opportune moment to give a Wet Willy to Lawrence and that's when the stuff really hit the fan.

I was in the middle of pondering many things (not the least of which was why I was in the car with these hellions in the first place) when things got out of control. Captain Patience remained at the helm and as composed as a skipper on scotch. He was fixated on the road, hands on 10 and 2, and he couldn't have been any calmer if he'd been sleeping.

Meanwhile, my patience went out the window like a bad habit. The fight in the back seat had escalated to epic proportions and left me with little or no choice but to pull out the big guns. "Don't make your father pull this car over!" I shouted, as if the mere mention of it would have them crouching in fear.

Just then Huey hurled a cookie. It ricocheted off of Lawrence's temple and hit Little Charlie square on the nose. Charlie, who had been minding his own business up until this point, took the hit personally and swung low and hard. Although he had full intentions of connecting with Huey's head and high hopes of doing some damage, he missed. Charlie then went full steam ahead into Vernon, who had been sleeping with head phones on and was most likely dreaming about "Eight Seconds on a Bull Named Fu Man Chu."

"I've had enough!" I said as I threw my *Guide to Better Parenting* magazine down on the floor. I leapt over the front seat and dove straight into the back section of the car in retribution.

I pulled Charlie off of Vernon and forced Huey and Lawrence back into their respective corners as I hissed and screamed with a vengeance. In fact, I'm quite certain they felt the vibrations as far north as Montana.

"Well," I said to my husband as I returned to the front seat and buckled my seatbelt, "What do you have to say for yourself?"

"Myself? What did I do?"

"You just sat up here and remained patient, that's what you did. It's a miracle that you can live with yourself after a performance like that."

"You know," he said with a calm smile, "you are absolutely right."

The nerve of that man.

2

GOLF

Way back in the days of Barney and mud pies, the kids thought I was the smartest woman alive. I was brilliant in their eyes. I was the guru who could educate them, make them wise, and show them the ways of the world.

Then they tossed out the dinosaurs and muck pastries and replaced them with sporting goods and athletic devices. Their interest turned from things I could comprehend and concepts I could conceive to events that would require them to throw balls and knock the tar out of each other.

Contrary to popular belief, being a mother of four boys doesn't automatically make one a sports expert. I can vouch for that. Due to my lack of knowledge and experience, their belief in my brilliance took the first Brain Train out of town and I was back to learning.

Adorned with the proper sports viewing attire and the right shade of lipstick, the bulk of my time has been spent in the stands. I nestle in with the other parents, look the opponents in the eye, and challenge them to "bring it on." Then I shyly look at the sports fan next to me and whisper, "What game are we playing and why?"

I've spent many hours watching the kids compete. I chomp on popcorn, enjoy a good beverage, and strive to understand. After many years of suffering with windburn, dehydration, and bleacher butt, I am finally beginning to catch on.

I've even begun to learn how to cheer like a

veteran and can scream with the best of 'em. "C'mon defense! Get your head in the game!" and "Box out, boys!" At a basketball game last winter I even got brave enough to shout out to a referee, "Call it both ways, buddy."

Sports took the spot where dinosaurs used to be—like an unwanted guest that moved in, stayed too long, and took over my life. I've had to learn to co-exist with the noisy existence of basketballs. I've grown numb to footballs careening past my head at warp speed. Even the threat of a baseball that dares to make an inside appearance no longer rattles my cage.

Then the eldest did as the oldest kid will often do. He went and introduced a whole new concept just to keep me on my toes—the ever loving and ever complicated world of golf.

Just when I thought I had things down pat with touchdowns, free throws, and home runs, the eldest started talking about eagles, birdies, and mashies. It's taken the better part of a decade for me to catch on to illegal motions and man to man defense. Now suddenly I'm supposed to understand double bogies?

When I asked him how he did at the end of his first practice, he made no sense whatsoever.

"Well, I scored a four under par on eight and I got an eagle on 13."

"Oh no! Was he hurt?"

"Who?"

"The eagle?"

"You don't have a clue, do you?"

"Don't mess with me, little mister. I've already forgotten more about fourth down and long than most moms will ever know."

Although I was reluctant to attend a golf match, I thought perhaps it'd help me learn more about the sport. I dressed appropriately, gathered all of my best sports-viewing-garb, and headed out to the course. I was busily seeking out the concession stand when my eldest came running at me from across the greens.

"OH, THERE YOU ARE!" I shouted. "HANG ON, HONEY. I'M ON MY WAY!"

I saw him cringe from afar so I loudly inquired, "WHAT? WHAT HAVE I DONE?"

"You can't shout here," he whispered as I approached. "In fact, you're not even supposed to talk."

"You're messing with me, right?"

"Mom, you have to be quiet so others can concentrate when they're putting."

"Whatever will I do with my blow horn?"

"Put the dang thing away. And you won't need your stadium seat or that corny banner either." He was looking at me with disgust as he added, "Do you have to wear that button with my picture on it?"

Taking after my mother, I replied, "You're breaking my heart! You know that, don't you?"

The strong winds pummeled at my being for the better part of an hour. I experienced solemn and somber moments as the golfers quietly hit one ball after another. Can't you just feel my pain?

There was no laughter, no high-fives, and heaven forbid an excited mother would shout, "Way to go, offense!" when her child connected with the ball.

Quite frankly, I've attended funerals with more action and excitement. With any luck he'll give up this spectator's sport and go back to his·dinosaurs. There's little chance of it I know, but a mother has a right to dream.

That's just par for the course.

3

THE PURSE

Way back in my single days I fancied a small purse. With color coordination as my game and fashion as my name, I carried only what I needed to get me through my average day.

Somewhere between diaper bags and athletic events, my handbag went through a dramatic change. One minute I was sporting a small alligator bag with a cute little clasp, the next thing I knew I was slinging an oversized, water-resistant satchel adorned with ducks and safety pins.

What was once a fashion statement turned into a ball-and-chain. It was almost like a prison sentence where I was doomed to carry everything my family needed. Bug repellents, Band-Aids, Chapstick, and sewing kits. Heaven forbid they'd tear their britches and I'd not be prepared.

It was hard to go from event to event as I struggled to find adequate seating to accommodate not only myself, but a purse that weighed close to three hundred pounds. Most of the time I would barely sit down before the first child would appear and announce that he was hungry. Without batting an eyelash, I'd pull out a box of Cheese Nips and a large bottle of spring water.

Before long I was not only supplying for my family, but for the needs of others as well. "Bobby has a headache, and Billy hurt his hand. They'll need some medicine and what do you have for a sunburn?"

"Well, I'm fresh out of my homeopathic remedy. But I do have a tube of Aloe Vera ointment. Ask Bobby if he wants Ibuprofen or Tylenol. If he can wait a minute I'll pull out my lab kit and we'll do a stat CBC and a Chem-7."

Things had really gotten out of hand.

Then one day I saw a woman on TV. She checked her lipstick and ran her fingers through her hair. Then she picked up a purse the size of a postage stamp and went out the door looking like a goddess.

Suddenly I wanted to be a goddess. I wanted a sleek look and a new design. I wanted to be a lady on the go. And I wanted to do so by simply grabbing a small bag that held only what I and I alone would need for the day.

I was tired of being a Walgreens on two legs and an ATM machine that doubled as a traveling companion. I no longer wanted to be the roadside first-aid center with supplies for the wounded and forlorn.

So I just went out and I did it. For a mere ten dollars and ninety-five cents I purchased the purse of my dreams. I was giddy with joy as I stood back and gazed upon my new handbag from afar. It glistened, it shone, and it simply screamed imitation Gucci.

I pulled a small mirror out of it and checked my lipstick. I didn't even have to rummage through the rubbish or dig to the bottom. I was thrilled with my new downsized existence. Then I flung my petite purse over my shoulder and hopped into the car where my first-born son greeted me with displeasure.

"What the heck is this?" he said as he held my new pouch up by its little strap. "A new miniature purse? Does Dad know?"

"Your father is so not the boss of me," I replied with more confidence than I felt. "I can have a new purse if I want to."

I went through the same thing with the 14-year-old, the 12-year-old, and the youngest who felt a personal betrayal at my having changed my lifestyle without first having checked with him.

"Where will you keep my chewing gum?" he asked through tears. "And what about my turtle food and Tyrannosaurus Rex?"

Within the week my reputation as a good mother went from being sub-standard to way below par. I'd been caught at sporting events without sunscreen. I'd let down a friend with halitosis and actually had no Kleenex when a kid sneezed at church. I was left with no choice but to put my cute imitation Gucci back on the shelf and to go back to my ball-and-chain—the over-sized satchel.

Yesterday I hoisted my bag up and plunked it down on a park bench beside me as I watched the kids play. Before long a poor soul came limping across the lawn as she dragged a bag that was as large as mine.

She skipped the introduction as she looked at my purse. "How long you in for?" she asked without missing a beat.

"With good behavior," I told her, "I should be out of this thing in about twelve years."

4

LUNAR CALENDAR ADJUSTMENTS

Summer vacation is just around the corner and I'm shaking in my boots. I can barely cope as I ponder the changes my life will undergo. Why, the brutal abuse my nerves will have to withstand alone is enough to make me cry *uncle*.

It could only be a matter of days before men in white jackets pull up to the curb to wrap me in a straight jacket and haul me away. And if it were to a place with clean floors and a tranquil environment I wouldn't even mind it much. In fact it might be just what the doctor ordered.

According to the calculations the children have made, only 14.5 days of peace remain. Less than fifteen short-lived spans of time to enjoy the peace and harmony their absence brings before they are back home with me for some serious twenty-four and seven action.

I shudder to think.

I was really starting to get the hang of spending time alone, too. The house has been so quiet during the day that I've actually heard sounds that I'd never heard before—like the ticking of the clocks, for instance, and the voices of the actors on my favorite soaps.

The toilets have stayed flushed, the shoes stay put away, and from 7:45 until 3:15 each day I can count on my can of Diet Coke staying right where I put it. I've even been able to consume an entire lunch all by myself.

It seems like just yesterday that I armed my despondent children with crisp new crayons, pencils, and tablets. In the midst of their grief I had tried to encourage them by purchasing the best sneakers that $19.99 would allow.

But the kids couldn't be bought.

Even the idea of a new protractor couldn't console them. As we approached the school their eyes were filled with tears. Their hearts were heavy laden and the very thought of sitting at a desk sickened them. Still, I sent them off with a smile and toted them off to all the training and education they could handle.

Bada-bing, bada-boom! My world turned full circle. Suddenly it's the end of the school year and the tables have turned. All the yucking it up I did in the fall has come back to bite me on the hind side. And they're not afraid to rub it in.

"Hey, Mom! Guess what! Since the last day of school doesn't really count, we only have fourteen days left. Can you even stand it?" Then they chant it over and over: "Fourteen days, Fourteen days, Fourte-e-e-n days!"—followed by tail wagging and the ever loving, "Oh yeah!"

The other day I got so sick of it that I had to dishearten one of them with a little creative dialogue.

"Honey, didn't you hear the bad news?"

"What bad news?"

"Well, your principal called and it turns out the school year will be extended by another month due to the LCA."

"The LCA?"

"Yeah, the Lunar Calendar Adjustment. See, they try to keep the annual calendar on track with the moon and the stars and all sorts of terrestrial stuff. They have to add a month now and then to even things out a bit. It's sort of like a Leap Year thing." At first I thought I'd lost him at "terrestrial," but then I noticed the look of raw fear as it appeared on his face. I smiled in spite of myself and nodded as I inquired, "Isn't that great?"

"Lunar Calendar Adjustment?"

"Yep, the good old LCA. So for all intents and purposes, it's really only the beginning of April." And with that he ran screaming from the room. Within a matter of minutes he'd summoned his younger brother, a couple of neighborhood kids, and a stray dog. Although he mispronounced *lunar*, he explained the LCA like a professor of doom.

"It's just like a stinking Leap Year or something like that, so now we have to do April all stinking over again. Doesn't that just stink?"

And with that, his little audience ran screaming from the room. Some ran to the TV for late-breaking developments. Others began to scour over the newspapers in hopes of finding information to discredit the story.

But the nine-year-old took matters into his own hands and went straight to his mentor. The guru of things true and untrue—the proficient older brother—who laughed, scoffed, and said, "Yeah, she tried to pull that one on me last year."

Alas, the jig was up. I knew it couldn't last, but I enjoyed myself just the same. Some may think me brutal. Others may scoff at my principles. But I tell you this—as far as I'm concerned, a Lunar Calendar Adjustment would be just what the good doctor ordered.

5

TIME TO TOSS THE DRAB

From the looks of what I saw on television the other night, the new summer line is out and it's fantastic. Turns out bright and bold colors are the way to go. We, as women, are to toss out the drab and the dreary. We are to get into the lime greens, bright oranges, and sunshiny yellows. According to the commercial, beautiful women everywhere couldn't be any happier with their new colors without breaking into song.
    Naturally, I too wanted to experience bliss. I wanted to don bright slacks and citrus colored scarves, layer up a couple of honeydew melon tanks, and walk in the sunshine. But I inventoried my closet and found that I have no melon colored Capri's. I have no citrus tanks. AND I was totally bummed when I realized that I owned not one pair of kiwi colored sandals. I was a disgrace not only to myself but also to women everywhere.
    I felt like a slob as I wondered what I wore last summer. Did I outgrow it? Did I grow tired of it? Or did all my fun clothing form conjugal unions with the missing socks before heading off to Mexico and a freer existence.
    It was quite obvious. I would have to do some shopping and do it quick. I could not be the only gal on the baseball diamonds this summer who was drab enough to be seen wearing dull colors and dreary khaki's. Wardrobe purchases would simply have to be made.
    As any veteran wife will tell you, the best way to drop the "I'm so spending money" bomb on a hus-

band is with dull commentary. I like to start with something that bores him to tears and then slip my little bombshell in between the sentences.

It's quite a clever method really. I waited until he was engrossed in a basketball game before I started with, "Honey, I've been thinking of some new methods for adding compost into my herb garden (generally I lose him at compost). I'm also considering basil this year and perhaps I'll bring in some color. I hate my clothes and anticipate it will cost us upwards of a couple hundred dollars before I am happy with my wardrobe again. By the way, what are your thoughts on sage?"

(Incidentally, this tactic also works splendidly for, "I may or may not have made a mathematical error in regard to the balance on the checkbook and it seems as though we may be overdrawn.")

Following his predictable "whatever you think," I headed to the department stores. I could see the brightly colored clothing from afar. I was eager with anticipation and giddy with joy at the prospect of what I might find. It was only when I got closer that that I realized that today's outfits are designed with only Britney Spears and her people in mind. The blouses would never have made it over my head and the slacks were small legged, low cut, and sported zippers shorter than my patience.

"Excuse me," I said to the gum-popping clerk as she passed. "Where are your shorts for women who may want to cover up more than 3% of their legs?" She just stood there looking at me as if a further explanation were needed. "Let's say, just for kicks and grins, that my thighs are actually bigger than my wrists. Is there a department here in your store that could actually clothe me?"

"Well yes," she finally replied, "we have a sarong section over in the corner, and if you have no luck there I could show you our catalogue. You'll love the new summer designs in our Gigant-o line."

"But what if I don't want to wear a tablecloth or a sarong or what ever you called it. What if I want to wear shorts? What if I want to give up my browns and blacks and step out wearing something bright and happy?"

She didn't say much else, but I felt her staring at my saddlebag hips and flabby upper arms indicating the bright and bold colors of the season were not for me.

I suppose she had a point. But she cannot control me. The slim cut kiwi colored Capri's may be out of reach for my physique, but that has nothing to do with footwear. And the melon colored sandals I'll be sporting this year are to die for.

6

NO MORE PENCILS, NO MORE BOOKS

If what the kids are saying is true, they are going to be out of school for the summer in a couple of days. That means I'm going to have to stock up on aroma therapy candles, brush up on my yoga, and find a place to hide out. Mum's the word. Last time I tried to hide out they joined me and inquired as to whom it was we were hiding from.

It just seems like yesterday that I dropped the little dears off with their crisp new supplies and backpacks. They fought back tears as they joined their peers, and I turned my face towards the sun and gave the day a five-mile smile.

These past nine months went by like a whirlwind. Sadly enough, the ball of agony is once again in my court.

"Mom, how many days do you suppose we have left of school now?" the oldest smugly inquires on a daily basis. "Would you be inclined to guess that it's less than ten? Well it is. Actually it's more like four and a half days. That's right, four and one half short and sweet days, for those of us who are counting. And you know *I* am."

Yesterday the younger kids took to doing the Bunny Hop through the house with floaties around their waist and swim fins on their feet. Chanting out, "S-U-M-M-E and R— all right!" as they went.

"Say boys," I said in an attempt to dampen their spirits, "anyone conjugate any verbs today?"

"No," the kindergartner replied with goggles on his face and a sea creature's fin atop of his head, "but how's my sunscreen look?"

"Like you slapped large globs of it all over your body. Where do you people think you're going?"

"We're getting ready to head to the lake. Can we go now? We'll let you use our reptilian swimming claws."

Although I won't readily admit it to the children, I'm not completely bummed that the school year is winding down. In fact, I've been feeling that if it doesn't end soon I may snap.

Some mothers love to help with the children's homework and I certainly am not one of them. Personally, I find their projects to be intrusive to my time. I've had it with the portfolios, dissertations, and essays. We've yet to complete the thesis paper that is due for science class.

"Your father is the science guy." I stated as I tried to get out of it. "I'm more of an English person myself."

"I don't think so." My son replied. "You've always been English *and* science. Besides, you're the writer."

"Yeah but who writes for science class? Why in my day, science was about test tubes and rocks."

I haven't always been so loathe to the idea of homework. When the oldest child had a project about cells in the fifth grade, I was quite eager to assist. I did research on the Internet, made models out of clay, and (to earn him extra points) I even dressed him up like a nucleus.

I showed far less enthusiasm for the second child. By the time the third child came along I'd completely run out of steam. I handed him my *Book of Life for Self Starters* and told him, "Hang in there little buddy."

This week alone we have thirteen final exams facing us. Along with a 3-D medieval castle that's due any minute and one mud-packed, sulfuric-acid volcano under construction. I begged Mrs. Dodson to let the idea go as I remembered the eruptions of volcanoes past, but she wouldn't bend. "It's what they'll remember about the third grade long after they've gone on to high school," she replied with a smile.

"How's about you change directions and go a different route this year?" I suggested as a last chance attempt. "Let them remember you for your award winning smile and unending wit. Oh! I know, how's about you let them remember you for that gnarly states and capitals test you gave them last January? I'll even bake a cake in the shape of Montana."

Yes sir-ee, it seems as if the teachers like to save all the "fun" for the end of the year. They like to give the arm of time a twist until parents cry out "uncle". And I'll be the first in line to scream it out. "Uncle!" "Aunt!" and if you need, "Cousin Annabellellen!"

I think I'm going to hide out in the back of my closet with an aroma therapy candle for a while.

Mum's the word.

7

WARNING: THIS GAL STOPS AT ALL GARAGE SALES

My name is Lori and I'm addicted to garage sales. It's true, I simply can't help myself. The prospect of buying someone else's used wares at discount prices is simply more than I can resist.

Today I own more burping plastic containers than a Tupperware distributor. I have shoes in every size and color, and a better variety of vacuum cleaners than the Kirby man. I have three blenders that won't operate, an electric skillet that's missing a leg, and a clock in the kitchen that sports a piece of masking tape that says *needs work*.

My family has been in love with garage sales since long before I was born. My people can smell used house wares from miles away. They've been known to wait in lines, scale fences, and park between the shrubs to be the first customers to appear.

Like any individual who suffers an addiction, I have no restraint. I stopped going to garage sales for awhile in order to regain some self-control.

Thinking I was cured, I slowly eased up to a garage sale last week and tried to remain composed. Suddenly my mouth started to water and my vision began to blur. I looked at the tables stacked with commodities, linens, and mismatched glasses until it became more than I could take.

"Okay Lori," I said out loud as I tried to keep my dignity, "you are only here to buy the things you need, and you need very little. You are only here to browse."

Yet once I saw that box of mismatched Melmac dishes marked down to fifty cents a cloud came over me, "what's one little purchase gonna hurt?" I asked myself.

Just then two fellow addicts began to argue over an 8-track that was billed as *like new*.

"Do you want a piece of me?" the larger one asked as she gave the 8-track a tug.

"Honey, I will slice you, dice you, and thump you like a melon."

I have no eight-track tapes, nor do I have a desire to listen to one. But suddenly and without warning a voice that may or may not have belonged to me said, "I'll give you each $2.50 to hand me the eight-track, turn your backs, and walk away."

Twenty minutes and a suburban full later, I drove off into the sunset with a smile wondering to myself if there was a system somewhere that transfers CDs to eight-track cassettes.

As much as I am a Garage Sale Queen, my husband is the Anti-king. He loathes the idea. Just the thought of spending money for unneeded and pre-used items is more than he can tolerate. Especially when one must make quick decisions in regard to something so enticing as plastic tumblers before another garage saler snatches it from you.

My husband could never shop so impulsively. The man thinks there should be a three-day waiting period before purchasing socks.

Meanwhile, I'm hanging out in someone's garage saying, "Here's an electric wok for a buck seventy-five. Do you think we can talk her down?"

It's not just me. My good friend Mabel is just as addicted as I. Last week we pulled into Mabel's driveway with a car loaded down with used goods. "I'm so glad Clark isn't home," she said as we hauled the purchases up to her door. "I'll have to hustle and bustle and get this all stashed before he gets back."

"What are you going to do with the lawn chairs, the overstuffed sofa, and this three legged chair?" I asked.

"I'm not sure," she replied. "All I know is that I couldn't just let them sit there for that price."

"And what about this stuffed Iguana?"

"Oh that," she said with a smirk, "I plan to give it to Clark for our anniversary. He's gonna hate it but what's a girl to do when an item such as this in the free box? Perhaps I'll tell him it's a symbol of our undying love."

We were each on an end of a large box of Harlequin Romance novels when we noticed that Clark was not at work as we had thought, rather he was in the living room and fully aware of Mabel's newly acquired junk. "Honey," Mabel said as she swallowed hard with surprise, "you're home?!"

I set down my end of the box and ran. Mable is my friend and all, but when it comes to consequences, it's every addict for herself.

8

THE WAGONEER

It's only a matter of months before our oldest child turns sixteen. Six short, racing-past-me months before that kid grabs the keys and heads out on his own, never to be seen or heard from again.

I still have nightmares about the first time I saw him round the corner on his Hot Wheels alone. The thought of it scared me half to death. By all rights he should still be in grammar school. He should still think Santa is real. He should believe that the tooth fairy is a cash cow with a fetish for teeth and that an over-sized Rodent hops through the house every Easter laying chocolate eggs and marshmallow Peeps.

He doesn't care about these things anymore. He's become fixated on cars and anything that looks good in a chrome bumper. Paying no mind to gas mileage or breaking his mother's heart, he talks constantly about independence and driving off into the sunset.

He has decided that the car of his dreams is the Jeep Wagoneer. With its fake wooden panels down the sides, a Tomken front receiver bumper with quick disconnects, and a glistening luggage rack, the Wagoneer would be his one way ticket to paradise.

"Just think, Mom, I'd have room for all of us kids and your groceries to boot. I could be a one-man delivery service and bring you all the milk that your heart desires. I'd take the kids to baseball practice, I'd run your errands, and free up your time. With the Wagoneer I could do it all. I'd even let you borrow it anytime you'd like to look like the coolest mom around."

"Frankly," I replied, "I'd feel a little safer running your brothers myself and I feel I look cool enough in my loaded down and dirty Suburban."

"Yeah, but," he quickly retorted, "Eddie O'Brien says the Wagoneer is as close to magnificence as I may ever come. He says it would lead me to greatness. Most of all, Eddie says the Wagoneer is a babe magnet."

Just what I need—a sixteen-year-old driving a babe magnet.

If I had my way he'd revert back to his Match Box Cars and spend the better part of his day making *vrooom-vrooom* noises with his lips and a make believe carburetor.

The need to drive is an obsession with him. I can't get out of the house without him. Just yesterday as I grabbed my keys and was tippy-toeing towards the door, he leapt into my path like a cat.

"I'll drive you."

"I don't need a driver. I'm very young and am perfectly capable of driving myself."

"But you work so hard. It's the least I can do."

"No, the least you could do is to fold a load of towels, find the remote for your father, and leave the driving to us."

"Mom," he said as he put a fist to his heart with great drama, "let me do this for you."

Once he was behind the wheel he began to mess with the music. He pulled my Led Zeppelin CD out of the player faster than you can say *Good Times Bad Times* and replaced it with a CD which contained men rambling on in a language I could barely understand.

"What is he saying?" I asked as I turned it down.

"Isn't it cool?"

"Is it English?"

"It's Jamaican."

"Don't they speak English in Jamaica?"

"Just sit back, Mom," he said as he shook his head in rhythm with the music. "Relax and leave the driving to me." Then he rounded the corner on two wheels and hit the curb.

"I only needed toilet paper and toothpaste." I shouted out over the music. "This is not a cause that one sacrifices their life for." An oncoming vehicle blared its horn before it swerved out of the way. "You're going to send us both to the great beyond. I'm not ready to die."

"Mom, you're like turning into a nervous wreck. You always go with the worst case scenario." I would have said something brilliant in response right then but the grip of fear wouldn't let me. "Let go of the door handle, Mom. Pull your foot back out of the floor boards and just enjoy the ride. Eddie O'Brien says it's the driving that makes the man."

"Who is this Eddie O'Brien character?"

"Eddie is a guy in the know."

"Eddie may be a guy in the know, but I doubt he's aware of what it cost to keep a car insured and a mother on Prozac."

I need to find this Eddie kid—and real soon. I need to grab him by the shoulders and give him a good talking to. And if he pushes me too far, I'm going to place him in the car with my fifteen-year-old and then I'll watch him squirm.

9

CURRY'S CICADAS

Today when my youngest son, Charlie, brought in the mail, he loudly announced, "Hey Mom! There is a present in with these letters!"
"Is it mine?" I asked from the laundry room.
"I bet it's mine!"
"Who is it from?" I asked, taking the box from him. When I saw that it was from my husband's cousins in Virginia and addressed to me, I was giddy with joy.
 A lesser woman would have torn open the package then and there. But I'm one for savoring the anticipation. Rather than opening the package right away I set it on the kitchen table and decided to finish up a few things first.
 I'd recently sent the cousins a copy of my book. So naturally I thought they'd sent me a little something to celebrate. The box was too small to house a bottle of wine and too light to hold a bronze award from the Writers' Guild.
 So I kept thinking to myself, *what could it be?* Cousin Mary Ann shares my fascination for jewels. Could it be a broach? Perhaps Tom and Mary Ann had visited some far away place and found the perfect trinket. I envisioned a lovely rhinestone pin—perhaps in the shape of a keyboard.
 Suddenly, the anticipation proved to be too great. I poured myself a cup of coffee and sat down with the box and a pair of scissors as the children looked on.

"Back off boys," I said with excitement, "this present is mine."

"How do you know it's yours and not mine?" Charlie asked.

"Because it says *Lori* and not *Charlie*. That's how I know."

"Why are they sending you a present and not me?"

"I'm not sure," I answered as I ripped off the last piece of tape. "Perhaps it's because they love me more."

I looked inside the carton and saw a smaller silver box inside—sporting a department store label. My level of anticipation tripled. "Look boys, it says Nordstrom's on the side of the box."

"What does Nordstrom's mean?"

"It means it's for me. Now take a step back please and give your gift-receiving mother some room."

I suppose it was the smell that gave me the first clue that this gift was no broach. And when I pulled out a baggie packed with Cicada bugs, the kids all backed up with a big fat "EEEEWWW!"

"What is it?" my squeamish 12-year-old asked as he curled up his nose.

"Whatever it is," his brother replied sarcastically, "we all need to remember that it's Mom's."

"They're Cicadas," I replied feeling rather puzzled.

"Are they for your bug-loving friend, Ethel?"

"They are now."

Turns out good old Tom and Mary Ann are suffering an infestation of Cicadas there in Virginia and couldn't let this historical event pass without sharing some of their misfortune with my good friend, Ethel.

Avid readers may recall the column I wrote about Ethel and her obsession for bugs, insects, and anything from the Orthoptera family.

Can't you just feel my pain?

I quickly stuck them in the freezer—Nordstrom's box and all. Then I called Ethel to complain to her about how I suffer for her sake. She's an odd duck, that Ethel, and she was excited to say the least.

"Did you pin them right away? Are they mounted? Oh, you are so lucky. The Cicada only appears once every 17 years. That's a fantastic bug. What great cousins you have. Although I don't know them, I really like that Tom and Mary Ann a lot."

I'd planned on taking some of the much-envied Cicadas to the baseball game the next night. Thinking perhaps I'd give them to the kids who'd need them for their up and coming seventh grade bug collections. But Ethel convinced me otherwise, saying that these Cicadas are priceless and should be hoarded until our next child needs them in the summer of 2007.

She assured me that the extra Cicadas could be traded for the highest price at that time. Perhaps for a Granary Corn Weevil or even (darest we dream) a Sorrel pygmy moth.

Be still my beating heart.

Not only have I married into what could possibly be known as the strangest family around, but I, Lori A. Clinch, am now the proud owner of some rare, one-year-out-of-17, Cicada bugs.

And to think, I would have settled for a broach.

10

BENDING REBAR

My beloved husband and I have decided to build a new home in the country—a little place far away from it all—gentle breezes, tranquil nights, and the blissful sounds of cows as they moo in the distance.

Rural living sounded like a great idea—at least until my spouse informed me that I should assist with the construction of our new abode.

"Help with the building?" I whined, "Are you crazy? I have weak knees and split ends. The only thing I know about nails is that mine are in bad need of a manicure. I can't work construction."

"Sure you can. If nothing else, you can keep me and the boys company." Oh yeah, keeping our boys company while they swing hammers at each other sounds like a *great* idea for passing the time.

My husband used to be a perfectly good companion. He was the kind of guy who would open the doors for me and give me his coat when I was chilled. He'd fix me a sandwich, pour my coffee, and if the timing were right, he'd clear off the sofa so I could sit down.

Marriage changed all of that. Before long I was mulching the yard, caulking the tub, and pumping my own gas. Once he realized I knew that 10w-30 was oil, it was my job to get it changed. I became the small appliance repair technician and the electrician's apprentice. When the toilets backed up it was my name the kids called out.

I'm not a die-hard feminist but I do have my

principles. I know that I can do most things that a man can do—perhaps even better.

If I wanted to, that is.

A couple of Sundays ago, the afternoon was so hot you could have fried an egg on a cowbell. I found myself on our building site helping my husband bend rebar of all things. By all rights I should have been home in the air conditioning. I should have had a load of whites spinning out with the rinse cycle, and soft music on the stereo as I asked my darling son, "So do you want to take a ride on the Reading Railroad or what?"

Instead I was smack dab in the middle of a construction zone. The temperature was a hundred if it was eighty. The wind was blowing to beat the band and I had enough grit and coarse products on my body to replenish an 8' x 8' sandbox.

Not that my husband cared. He caught me taking a break from the work to remove tumbleweeds from my hair and said, "There are more wires that need to be tied."

"I don't want to tie more wires," I whined. "I've never wanted to be a construction worker—that's your world. We took vows during our wedding ceremony. I know we did. They went something like 'The man should work the land and the woman shall labor with children.' Well, I've labored, Little Mister. And I've got four boys as living, breathing proof that my labor is done. It's your job to till the soil. Besides, steel toed boots make my ankles look chunky."

I expected sympathy out of him—in the very least a little pity. Instead he gave me a pair of oversized vice-grips and walked away. "My nails are thinning even as we're speaking," I called after him. "My wrinkles are multiplying and it'll take a $30.00 conditioner to restore the luster to my hair. I don't belong on a job site miles away from a hot shower."

He stopped hammering for a moment, turned to me and said, "Your hair used to have luster?"

It's not as if we women can reverse the whole situation. As any female will tell you, just because we've changed the oil on the lawnmower and unclogged the back flow device, doesn't mean the men of the world are going anywhere near the hard water deposits on the kitchen faucet with a pumice bar.

Generally speaking, men are color blind when it comes to laundering the clothes. They believe fast food just magically appears on the table and think that *men with mops* sounds like a good name for a support group.

Yet I shall persevere. I shall rise up. I shall overcome. I could buy a cute hard hat—perhaps one with a convenient insulated bottom compartment that can be used to hold beverages, sandwiches and a woman's liberation magazine.

I could buy safety goggles, fashionable chore gloves, and pay one of the kids to spritz me with a little aroma therapy potion now and then. I could throw caution to the wind and tackle any task that comes my way. I could fight for women's liberation and show all of mankind that I, Lori A. Clinch, am capable of doing anything that a man can do—perhaps even better.

I just don't want to.

11

MAKING THE KIDS DO LAUNDRY

Summer vacation is in full swing. The counters are riddled with bowls of half-eaten cereal, beach towels are strewn about, and around every corner there's a child who mutters, "I'm bored," and "what are we going to do today?" as he slumps against a wall.

The food and the mess are one thing. But it's the laundry that's going to take me down for the count. I've been doing my best to beat it but it is a worthy adversary. I've been washing at odd hours, stopping home when I had an extra fifteen minutes to put another load in, and have recycled the boys' baseball uniforms on more than one occasion.

Still, the pile of soiled apparel has multiplied, divided, and conquered what used to be a nice living space. The shirts have doubled, the jeans have reproduced, and I'm quite certain that—when my back was turned—the socks went out and acquired new and unattached friends. I guess one never could trust socks to live out a monogamous existence.

"Where did this shirt come from?" I shouted out yesterday as I held up a bright turquoise-flowered Hawaiian garment. Near as I knew, we had no Hawaiian shirts. I'll bet the kids don't even know what a lei is, much less who Don Ho is.

"That's my shirt," said a child as he walked by munching on a bag of Funyuns, "I tried it on but I decided that it didn't go with my Nike shorts."

He may never make Mr. Blackwell's Best Dressed List nor will he become a slave to fashion, but at least he knows that he can't mix Nike with a Luau.

One day last week, as a form of self-encouragement, I counted down the years that I have left to do laundry for a family of six. I told myself—if one doesn't take sports wear into account—the old washer and dryer may actually have a day off in about eleven years.

Give or take.

When I related this good news to my good friend Sharon she proceeded to drop a sock bomb on me with a horror story about her college student who came home last month. Turns out the kid brought 18 loads of soiled laundry with him.

"I'd never seen anything like it," she said in disbelief. "I heard a beeping noise out on the front lawn and thought a semi-truck had mistakenly taken our house for a loading dock. I ran out to the front porch just in time to see my 19-year-old-son, Earl, backing up a truck that was filled to the hilt with dirty clothes."

"Earl doesn't do his own laundry?"

"No," she replied. "He saves it up until he has nothing left to wear but his skivvies and an old pair of gym socks."

Her story scared me straight. If her Earl was bringing laundry home, then it was quite possible that this may be a common thing. Like a detective on a mission I immediately began to make inquiries by calling every mother with college age children I knew. Had they done all they could? Had proper techniques been introduced? Had in-services been conducted and seminars attended?

Everywhere I turned, the story was the same. Kids left home, and when they returned, they brought their dirty apparel back with them. They brought home their khaki's, their capris, and their dungarees. They brought sweatshirts, t-shirts, smelly undergarments, and enough dirty socks to fill up Manhattan.

I had no choice. Although I hadn't let any member of the household touch the laundry since The Great Pink Load of 1997, it was time I took the bull by the horns.

"Line up men!" I called out to the bored group of young men who were strewn about the front lawn.

"Is it a chore?" whined the youngest.

"It's a form of independence," I replied with a smile. "Today is the day you boys will take your first step towards a freer existence. Today we're going to do a seminar entitled, *Your Dirty Clothing and You*. We're going to fold the towels, mate the socks, and—if I'm a woman who's worth half of her salt—you boys will be talking the language of fabric softener sheets by the end of the day."

As I walked away I gave myself a high five. "Go, Lori!" I said out loud and to no one in particular. I was dang proud of myself for having killed two birds with one stone. Not only were my little darlings going to relieve my burden, they finally had the answer to, "What are we going to do today?"

12

REMEMBER BAD CAR TRIPS?

It takes a brave soul to load up a car full of kids and head out of town. It takes a person of great demeanor, a courageous warrior who can rise up against the odds and smile in the face of adversity.

Yep, that's what the brave people do all right. Smart people just stay home.

Sadly enough, it would seem that my beloved spouse and I are neither brave nor smart. We're just middle-aged adults who had to get to a family reunion in Eastern Nebraska.

When we were first married traveling was much different. He'd drive while I browsed through magazines in an attempt to learn how to decorate the bathrooms with a creative flair. On one such occasion I actually got bored with elegance and grace. So, just for a little entertainment, I decided to make my newly wedded husband squirm with the proverbial, "Do you love me?"

Men just hate that sort of questioning.

"Yep," he replied as he began to fidget.

"How much?" I asked with a batting of the eyelashes.

"Why must you torture me?"

"It's a simple question."

"Okay, I love you lots. What kind of junk are you reading in those magazines anyway?"

"Tell me," I said as I scooted closer, "tell me why you love me?"

"Lots of reasons."

"Just tell me one."

"Okay, you have a nice personality."
"A nice personality? That's it? That's what folks say about ugly people. You may as well say, 'with the right sack for her head she'd be quite a catch'."
Those were the days. Magazines, discussions, and lovers' spats. And those car rides were nothing like our most recent road trip.
I knew before we pulled out of the garage that things were going to get ugly. Yet, the family reunion called. And what better reason to take a road trip than to visit our gene pool and showcase our little dears.
Before we'd rounded the first corner, the youngest made a sound that was reminiscent of a missile going off at 3 a.m. It was a high pitched sound that certainly could have shattered windows as far as Texas. It certainly shocked the socks right out of my cerebellum.
"What did you do to him?" I demanded as I turned in my seat to face the brawl.
"Nothing," replied the guilty party, "he just started bawling."
"He keeps touching me," the youngest cried out in between sobs. "He pulled my hair, and he said I was a little girl."
"Are you a little girl?"
"No."
"And if you were a little girl would that be a bad thing? Cuz I gotta tell ya, I was once a little girl and it was really quite nice."
"He touched me first," replied the instigator, ignoring my statement.
"Well, for gosh sakes knock it off and don't touch each other any more."
We'd barely traveled ten miles before they started in again. They picked, they pinched, and they

made the youngest scream. My patience declined at a rapid rate and my hands began to tremble.

Then the eldest joined in by placing his feet directly into his brother's face. The next thing I knew the older two children were going at it with such violence I considered contacting Don King and telling him we had fighters and could certainly use a promoter.

They screamed, they hollered, and they made me so mad that I started screaming back. In a tone that would have appalled Mothers' groups world wide, I threatened them with loss of life and limb and a homeless existence.

The thought of pulling over and putting them out on the curb sounded pretty gosh darned tempting.

Then it happened. It was like a rainbow after the hurricane. Somewhere between the cornfields and the wide expanse of the great valley, they fell asleep. I don't know how, I don't know why, but I knew better than to question the powers that be. I simply took it as a sign that there is a God and that He does love me.

I whipped my magazines out faster than you can say pish-posh and bling-bling. After leafing through a few pages I decided that bathrooms with a creative flair really aren't all they are cracked up to be.

"Honey?"
"Yeah."
"Do you love me?"
"What do you think?"
"I think if you still love me for my personality we're in a lot of trouble."

13

TURNING FORTY

It just seems like yesterday that my mother turned forty. I can still remember how she loudly announced to anyone who would listen that although she'd still welcome gifts she most definitely was not having any more birthdays. She made it quite clear that she loathed the idea.

My siblings and I took it as a sign that she needed a party—and a big one. We invited everyone she knew and a couple of people she had forgotten about. We purchased black balloons, put denture crème in grab bags for the guests to take home, and hung a big sign out back that said, "Oh no, Mom's a big fat four-Oh."

We dressed the guest of honor in a comfy housedress, a blanket, and some slippers. Then we set her in a chair and wheeled her to the patio where she could "enjoy the breeze."

"Forty is not old!" she said in protest.

"Careful Mother," warned my sister, "you don't want to upset yourself. Remember your heart condition."

"I don't have a heart condition, you fools. I have my real teeth and I'm still using cheap moisturizers."

"Just the same, we wouldn't want you to get too winded. Hows about another glass of Metamucil, dear? Or do you think it's time we switched to prune juice?"

It was the best *over-the-hill party* ever. We put the emphasis on *old* and chuckled to ourselves with disbelief that forty-year-old people still thought they *could* party.

Now, thanks to the passing of time and the winds of change, my fortieth birthday is looming in the distance. It's like a big hammer of doom that's bound and determined to come smashing down on my tower of youth.

I tried to come to grips with it by saying, "I'm forty" in the mirror a couple of times. It still didn't seem to be a good fit. I took to saying it stern and matter of fact, even putting descriptive words here and there. "I'm going to be forty," "I'm pretty much going to be forty," "I am just barely forty. Forty-something, forty-ish, hardly out of the thirty-something age range."

I started saying, "I am almost forty," to anyone who would listen. I said it to friends, tele-marketers, and the gals at the grocery store. Last week I stood up in the middle of a public gathering and loudly announced, "My name is Lori and I'm facing an end of an era."

It would be easier to deal with the onslaught of a new decade if others didn't make me feel so old. The jokes never seem to end. For instance, I asked my good friend Mabel to pass me the carrots the other day. "Why bother?" she said as she pushed a stack of cookies my way, "Forget the health food. At your age you need all the preservatives you can get."

My father has taken to referring to me as an old woman, the children keep telling me to remember the "*good old days*", and my good friend Karen has warned me not to start any long novels.

In fact, Karen told me that my mind would be the first thing to go—followed by my skin, hair, eyesight, and finally my ankles.

"What's going to happen to my ankles?" I asked with fear.

"You remember those slouch socks you wore in the '80s that bunched all around your calves, don't you?"

"Yeah?"

"Well one day, you're going to awaken to realize that your skin has created the same look for you. It's a real mess. In fact, now that you're turning forty you'll find that you'll stoop to tie your shoes and you'll wonder what else you can do while you're down there."

"How's about if I get into shape, run a few laps, and take a neuroMod memory course?"

"Won't help," she insisted. "With your fortieth birthday rapidly approaching, it's only a matter of time."

"Only a matter of time until what?"

"How should I know?" She replied, "I turned forty years ago. I don't remember these things." Then she paused for a minute, took on a blank stare, looked at me and said, "Say girl, were you talking or was I?"

Didn't that just tickle my aging funny bone?

Well, I for one am not going to take this sitting down. I'm going to call my mother and tell her that she was right—forty is most definitely not old. In fact forty is still dang young! I'm going to rise up and do something about it. Take the bull by the horns. Show this age thing who's the boss and party with the rest of them. And I will too.

Just as soon as I've finished my Geritol and had my mid-morning nap.

14

POTTY TRAINING

My sister, Patti, called me the other day, seeking my advice. "Say kid," she said, "I'm trying to make a decision about a potty seat. I think it's about time to train little Johnny."

I darn near sprayed my coffee. Potty training little Johnny would be a test for any mother— even one as stellar as Patti. That little man is a poster child for the terrible two's. He sports a mischievous grin, chubby ankles, and fat little hands that are always full of something he shouldn't have: blunt instruments, crumbled cookies or—heaven forbid— the dreaded black Sharpie marker. He's a one-man destruction team that can change any décor into Early American Demolition with less than a single passing of a room. To be honest with you, I felt so sorry for her that I could have cried.

"I just don't think I can put it off any longer," she continued as if reading my thoughts. "He's two and a half, his little sprinkler comes on with great frequency, and heaven knows he's shown enough interest in flushing."

I gave her my opinion on toilet seats and hung up with a promise to go down to the church first thing in the morning to send prayers in her direction.

When parenting was new to me, I was foolish enough to believe that potty training would be a snap. According to my *Journal of Knowledge for Better Parents*, all a good mother needed was a joyful disposition and a Tinkling Tunes potty-chair.

Armed with a smile and some good literature, I grabbed my little cherub and happily placed him on the throne. While we listened to rendition after rendition of Potty Time Sing Along songs, the precious dear unraveled an entire roll of toilet paper along with a week's supply of nerves.

Being young and not easily discouraged, I lovingly read him, *Your Potty Parts and You, The Guide to Regularity* by Dr. Hasnokids. The good doctor seemingly took great delight in falsely assuring gullible parents that potty training would not only be a fun and simple process, but that a good time would be had by all.

After the fifteenth rendition of potty training lyrics, I had an uncontrollable urge to smash the singing potty-chair into smithereens. Yet, being a woman of great endurance, I persevered.

"Let's try again tomorrow," I said with more enthusiasm than I felt. After all, Dr. Hasnokids recommended that we keep a positive attitude at all times.

The very next day, my child took to pulling off his diaper, and did so at every turn. Before long the peep shows became a constant and regular ritual. He did it in the yard, in church, and in the store. At any given moment, in an act of spontaneity, he'd entertain the neighbors and passersby as well as any unsuspecting guests.

It was back to the old drawing board. I tossed out my *Dr. Hasnokids Journal for the Gullible Parent*, and consulted my dear neighbors the Mimfords. Arlo and Buffy had been through potty training camp and assured me that success was just around the corner.

"Our little Marybell was expressing signs that she was ready to train by the age of one," Arlo said in a boasting and condescending voice.

"Yes," Buffy added with a confident flair, "we simply said 'tinkle, Honey' and she was ready to leave the world of incontinence behind."

Prepared to follow Buffy's lead, I sat my child back on the lavatory. Although I couldn't bring myself to say the word, "tinkle," I said a lot of other descriptive words that meant the same dang thing.

I received little or no results that rivaled the magnificent victory the neighbors experienced. Therefore, I decided then and there to terminate my relationship with the Boasting Mimfords. After all, life's too short to befriend parents who succeed vicariously through their children.

After visiting with Patti, I took a trip into the attic to do an inventory on my potty training gadgets and gizmos. I still had everything the experts had recommended. Including a Bobsy Won't Wetsy doll and a $20.00 singing chair. I had all it would take to inspire a child to join the "big boy" world and enough literature to stock an entire library on incontinence.

Keeping this in mind, I waited a few days before I called my sister. "Say girl," I asked as I poured a cup of coffee, "how's the potty training going?"

"Oh," she replied, "that lasted less than a day. I had good intentions, and they went out the window as soon as he took off his high dollar pull-ups and put them on his head. I don't suppose you have any suggestions, do you?"

"Beats me kid," I said as I thought of the Mimfords, "all of my kids trained overnight."

15

TELEMARKETERS

Sometimes I think life would be much simpler if it weren't for the telephone. My mother would have to drive across town to lay guilt trips on me, there would be no wrong numbers at 3 a.m., and our children would not be able to call me when I'm out to dinner to report that the oldest child had clocked them for no reason.

Best of all, a gal such as myself would be able to live out a telemarketer-free existence. Since my husband I have a business listing, we are prey for every telemarketer with a directory at his fingertips. They call during lunch, they interrupt my slumber, and I swear they have spies who report to them any time I scale a nine-foot ladder to replace a burned out bulb.

A while back, a telemarketer called as I was scrubbing the toilets. The woman was obviously under the misconception that we were a large corporation because she asked to speak to our marketing administrator.

Sporting a scrub brush in one hand and a can of Comet in the other I replied, "She's in a conference with the director of commodes at the moment. May I take a message?"

"Who am I speaking to?" she inquired in a business tone.

"This is Lori."

"Hi Lori, are you allowed to make decisions for the business?"

"Why yes!" I replied feigning enthusiasm.

"Just yesterday, following a meeting of the minds, I made the decision to buy a box of pencils all by myself!"

"Great! I'd like to ask you a couple of questions in regard to your purchasing department."

"Oh, then you'd definitely want to speak with our fifteen-year-old. Heaven knows no one can make purchases like that kid can. Unfortunately, he's tormenting the Department of Siblings at the moment and that is not a meeting one would want to interrupt."

Becoming annoyed with my little antics, she then asked to speak to whoever *was* in charge.

"Listen honey," I replied, "you must be under the misconception that we are a large firm. Truth is, we're basically a Ma and Pa organization. It's pretty much just him, me, a couple of guys, and a hammer."

"Oh, are you his wife?"

"Well, if he's Pa, then I guess that makes me Ma." With that, she hung up, leaving me—Director of Commodes—to scrub the bathroom alone.

The clincher of all phone calls came today, when an enthusiastic and chipper man called and inquired as to how the weather was in our parts. I knew right away what he was up to. Anybody who is that happy at 8:00 in the morning is either trying to peddle useless wares or has been nipping at the sauce.

"This is James West," he sang out as if he were a long lost buddy, simply calling to shoot the breeze.

"What are you selling James West?" I asked him point blank.

"Tools and supplies."

"We've got all the tools and supplies we need at the moment, Jim. We've got things that splice, grippers that vice, and should a bolt dare to release itself, we've a ratchet set that can tighten with the best of them. Now please remove us from your list and we'll call it a day."

James should have wished me well, thanked me for my time and re-dialed. Turns out that James was the pit-bull of telemarketers. Rather than be denied he simply replied, "No way."

I couldn't believe it. "Did you just tell me no way?"

"That's right," he replied, "I said, 'no way'."

Right about then the mother in me took over. I planted my fist firmly on my hip, stiffened my spine, and in my best no-nonsense tone I said, "You did not just tell me 'no way'."

"Oh yes I did."

"Oh yeah! Well, we'll see about that." I went from being aggravated to just plain mad. I wanted to scream. I wanted to jump up and down and pitch a fit. Most of all, I wanted to reach through the phone and shake some sense into this man. "Tell you what James, hows about if I call the Better Business Bureau and report you? Or better yet, I'll find out if there's a control center for telemarketers gone wild and then I'll have you incarcerated?"

"Yeah! Well, how about if I call you back every fifteen minutes."

"Oh yeah?"

"Yeah."

He seemed to know that he had me shaking in my boots because that dirty dog slammed the phone down on me.

He hasn't called me back yet. But I will tell you this—if James West calls again, I'm going to put him in direct contact with our Adolescent Litigant department.

That should make him rue the day.

16

I'M SORRY, WHO ARE YOU?

I've always admired people with a good and solid memory—the brilliant folk who can remember dates, places, and local events. I feel such people deserve applause, praise, and perhaps even a smack upside the head.

I'm especially jealous of the individuals who can remember names. They make the rest of us look bad. I once saw a woman like that on TV. She was a real brainiac who remembered the name of each and every person she had ever met. "How do you do that?" asked the interviewer.

"It's all in the vault," the woman replied, tapping her head.

That's a tough pill to swallow for a gal—such as myself—who's been known to call her very own offspring "little what's his face."

Oddly enough, the kids have learned to accept it and decided to stand by my side. It's a good thing too—I really need them around to help me find the car keys.

My friends, on the other hand, aren't quite as accepting of my shortcomings. Take for instance my good friend Toni who lives just up the street. Toni might even be her real name for all I know. Due to a glitch that has taken over my thinking centers, I often times call her Kati. However, I keep things on an even keel by calling my good friend Kati, Toni.

I just blame it on the glitch.

Last week I had a long and pleasant chat with Toni. After we'd discussed all of the issues we needed to (including stubborn stains and molding bread) I wished her well.

"I'll talk to you later, Lori," she said using my actual name. (She can be such a showoff sometimes.)

"Okay, Kati," I replied, and then I hung up the phone.

She instantly called me back and said, "You just called me Kati."

"Oh?"

"Kati," she repeated. "I said 'talk to you later, Lori' and then you replied 'Okay, Kati'."

"Do tell," I said, still not seeing what she was getting at.

"Lori, my name is Toni."

"Oh, that's right," I said as I finally realized the error of my ways. "I'll put that in the vault for next time." (As if my mental vault weren't a chamber full of holes with a faulty door.)

I asked my mother about it later over a cup of coffee, "Do you think it's me?"

"More than likely," she replied with brutal honesty. "Are you losing sleep?"

"Not so you could notice."

"Are you eating properly?"

"If you can count celery and Melba toast."

"That's your problem," she said as she slapped the table for emphasis. "It's a lack of nutrition for certain. Perhaps you should try a new regimen of vitamins. You should go out and buy yourself some of that Ginkgo Biloba."

"Oh yeah," I replied with all of the teenage sarcasm I could muster, "that's just what I need—more vitamins and extracts. Next thing I know you'll have me grinding herbs with a pumice bar."

My confusion with Toni and Kati came to a head just last week when I attended a Coddled Cook party that Kati was throwing. With Toni seated on one side of me and Kati on the other, I was happily watching the cheerful consultant as she cooked up a storm.

"The best news of the day," the consultant said with a smile, "is that Kati is going to join our company and become a Coddled Cook consultant!"

As the other gals gave a round of applause including cheers and whistles, I turned to Toni—once again confusing the names—and said, "Really?"

She said nothing and gave me a puzzled look. A few brief minutes later the consultant once again mentioned Kati's decision to join the fast paced world of efficient cooking.

"You too?" I said, this time turning to Kati.

"Yes Lori, she just mentioned it like two minutes ago. Weren't you paying attention?"

"Well, I heard that Toni was going to be a consultant, but I didn't know you had decided to do it, too."

"I'm not going to be a consultant," Toni blurted out.

"Oh," I replied. "Well, you'd better tell the consultant, Honey, because she's certainly convinced that you are!"

"Lori," someone asked later as the party was wrapping up, "have you ever considered taking the time to learn about memory stimulating vitamins such as Ginko Biloba?"

"Oh, I've studied plenty," I said with a meager smile. "I've learned bunches and it's all right here in the vault."

"Do you have a vault?" asked Toni sarcastically as she passed by.

"Yeah," I replied. "I just wish I could remember where I put the key."

17

MAMA TRIED BUT HER BOY LOVES COUNTRY

Back in my day, all of the *cool* kids listened to rock-n-roll. If there were any teenagers who were so square as to actually like country music, they'd never admit it outside of their home—it just wouldn't be safe for one's reputation.

My mother, on the other hand, was a great fan of country western. She loved Conway Twitty, Hank Williams, and anyone who could sing gospel music with a backwoods twang. Every so often we'd try to make her cool by forcing her to sing our songs. But we quickly learned that she was the only woman north of Oklahoma who could make an Aerosmith song sound as though it was being articulated by Loretta Lynn.

"I'm going to be cool to my kids," I once told her, "because I like rock-and-roll."

When my first child was born, he was drawn to the zippy sounds of Barney. "No-no Honey," I'd warn, as he'd sing along with that annoying purple dinosaur. "Listen here, this band is called Foreigner. Now isn't that better?" I felt proud that he was the only child in his pre-school group who could sing every word of "Juke Box Hero."

I also taught him Billy Joel, Billy Squire, and enough Led Zeppelin songs to make my mother doubt my sanity.

When he reached puberty, he began to branch out on his own. I expected as much and wasn't about to let a little rap music scare me off. I could still be cool. If rap music was what his generation was about, I could go with that. After all, that's what cool mothers do.

So, one day while he was at school, I listened to the words, and memorized a song, and got my music on. When he returned home from school later that day, I was mopping the floor as I rapped out about my homies and hanging with my boys.

"What are you doing?" he exclaimed as he walked into the kitchen.

"Whatsup?" I quickly replied to my disgusted child. "I've been gettin' down with my bad self all afternoon."

Making no attempt to hide his distaste, he shook his head and walked away. He must have decided then and there that if his mother were listening to his music, changes would have to be made. It wasn't long before I began to notice telltale signs that he was being drawn into a world where I'd never go.

Musically, that is.

I tried to deny it could be true, but on more than one occasion I found the TV on the Country Music Channel. I thought I heard the sound of a steel guitar coming from his bedroom. And once—when he thought I wasn't listening—I could have sworn I heard him yell out, "Yee-Haw!"

As mothers in denial are prone to do, I tried not to think about it and pretended this little problem didn't exist.

Then one day he pulled up with friends and the unmistakable sound of twang was coming out of the radio speakers. The confrontation was imminent. I had refused to believe it until it slapped me in the face.

"What on earth are you kids listening to?" I disgustedly asked my son.

"It's a cool song, Mom, just listen to the words."

"Turn that nonsense off before my friends drive by." It was a matter of principle.

Try though I may, I cannot dissuade him. Lately the car radio has been an object for all out war. Now-a-days my Janis Joplin is being interrupted by some blockhead singing out about 2.7 seconds on a bull named Fu-man-chu. That kid can switch the radio off of my classic rock station and onto the boot scootin' boogie faster than you can say *honky tonk*.

Worse yet, the other day I had to endure a woman as she blared out with pride that she's a redneck woman and not a high class broad.

Can't you just feel my pain?

My kid is sitting in the living room even as I write this. His headphones are on and he's singing about red dirt roads, pick-up trucks, and a dog named Bo.

I could still be a cool mom, if I really wanted to. I could join him in his music, and listen to it while he's out. Why, I could learn the words and get my western on. And if he asked me, "For the love of horses Mother, what are you doing now?" I could sing out with a twang that is reminiscent of my mother's, "Aw kissed him on the lips and left his be-hi-hind for you."

I guess I could. But I gotta be honest with you, I have no interest in being *that* cool.

18

SECOND THOUGHTS ON BACK TO SCHOOL

At the risk of sounding insane, I have to admit I am a little bummed that summer vacation is coming to an end.

Despite the fact that the cupboards are empty, the kitchen is in a perpetual state of Pandemonium, and the TV has been blaring non-stop for three days running, I almost hate to send my little dears back to school.

It just boggles the mind, doesn't it?

One would think the prospect of living out a child-free existence for 7.5 hours per day would have me dancing in the streets. But I'm not sure we've had the chance to enjoy the summer like we should have. Our trips to our favorite swimming hole were limited; we never—not even once—slept in past noon; and our one and only lemonade stand bombed like a lead balloon.

But that's what I get for trying to make entrepreneurs out of a bunch of rowdy, thirsty boys.

Still, the back-to-school ads are filling the mailbox and the school bells are going to ring whether I am ready or not.

But it all changed yesterday when I decided that I'd put off the inevitable long enough and that it was time to take action. I knew the old gym bags would need to be explored, school supplies would have to be located and—if I was to do it up right—someone was going to have to be brave enough to sort through the clothes.

Just the thought of opening the door to Huey's closet scared me half to death. I had been down that path before, and it was scary just to think of it. I must have stood and looked at it for twenty minutes as I tried to summon the courage.

Then I took a deep breath, braced myself, and pulled the doors back.

"Ah, c'mon!" I exclaimed with disgust. "Look at this place!" The clutter was overwhelming. It smelled like dirty gym socks, and some of my best dishes had taken a temporary refuge in there.

As any mother worth her salt would be prone to do in this situation, I summoned him loudly, being sure to use his middle name to show I meant business.

When my darling child appeared, I firmly inquired, "When was the last time you cleaned this thing out?"

"I believe," he said as he shoveled a handful of potato chips into his mouth, "the last closet cleaning session took place back when Little Charlie lost his pet turtle in here."

"That wasn't a cleaning session. That was a search and rescue. This place looks like a pigsty. I'll tell you what, Little Mister, I'll give you a half an hour and when I return I want this place ship-shape."

Not ten minutes had passed before he hollered out, "I'm finished!" I stepped into his room to see that he had taken everything out of the closet and piled it on the bed. All that was left in his closet was a pair of football cleats, an old t-shirt, and a small pile of potato chips.

"What is that?" I asked as I pointed to the immense mound of clothes, rubbish, and debris.

"That's the stuff I don't want."

"That rag hanging in the closet is the only thing you still like?"

"That's not a rag. That's my favorite football shirt."

I grabbed a stellar looking item from his discard pile—a blue shirt that was "to die for" last fall. "And what about this?"

"I hate that shirt."

"What do you mean you hate this shirt? Isn't this the shirt you just 'had to have' last October? The very shirt that in and of itself—and I quote—'made the difference between you and the man you were meant to be?'"

"Yeah, but it fits me funny. The arms are like all stupid and stuff."

"But you swore you couldn't live without it."

"Well, I didn't realize that it was going to be a life-long commitment." This I get from the child who was in tears because I threw away his artwork.

"What about these pants? There's nothing wrong with these."

"Those pants are like, so lame."

"Since when can pants be lame?"

"Ever since they made those pants."

It was the same with 90% of the clothing in his closet. By the time we were done, we had nothing left hanging in the closet but some old shoes, a couple of shirts that looked like rags, and the pile of chips.

That's what I get for getting maudlin when I should be celebrating. Now that the little session has ended, I've changed my mind. The quicker they go back to school the better. I may even take a well-deserved trip to the swimming hole without them.

19

SO MUCH FOR IGNORING THE PROBLEM

For reasons we may never understand, one of our little dears reached across the table during lunch last week and smacked his brother upside the old toboggan. Needless to say, his brother reciprocated the smack with a smack of his own. Of course that smack was followed by another smack, screams, cries, and a plethora of name-calling.

Rather than respond to the situation, my beloved spouse and I pretended to hear nothing. Having tried and failed at every other attempt to make them get along, we thought we'd try out step 463C of our *Parental Techniques Journal* entitled, "If You Ignore Them, They May Go Away."

I reacted to the altercation by taking a sip of my coffee and Pat simply turned to page two of the newspaper.

"Did anything exciting happen this morning?" he shouted at me as he tried not to look at the brawl that was taking over the kitchen.

"I found a quarter in the lint trap," I shouted back. Inside I was experiencing a break down of epic proportions, but I did my best to mask it and simply added crème to my coffee.

"A quarter," Pat shouted above the screams. "That sounds exciting. Will you invest it or add it to our slush fund?"

"I may just pocket it for now!"

Just then, the altercation picked up speed. The boys screeched, yelled, and pitched fits as we sat and pretended to be oblivious to it all.

"Did you see what he did?" one of the kids shouted out at no one in particular.

"He's an idiot!" another child exclaimed.

"I love you too, dear Brother," the eldest responded—which totally ticked the younger one off—so the brawl moved up a notch and went full steam ahead.

Although I was doing a fine job of masking it, I was at the end of my internal rope.

"I don't think this is working," Pat shouted as he folded up his paper. "I can't hear myself think."

"You're telling me," I responded. "I haven't heard the voices inside my head for over a month now."

Just then I noticed a Back to School ad lying on the table. "Looka here boys!" I loudly exclaimed as if we'd just won the lottery. "Cha-ching! It's an ad for backpacks, ink pens, calculators, and big pink erasers. Oh my goodness! The heavens are surely smiling down upon us today. The store has White-Out, protractors, and wide-ruled reams of paper. Some of it's only ten cents to boot! Why, that's a bargain at twice the price."

The brawl instantly ceased to commence and our two boys looked at me in dead silence. "They're selling glue for 19 cents," I continued, "and they're practically giving Fiskar scissors away," I added to drive the idea home.

"That's just mean," said my eldest child with great cynicism.

"Yeah," responded his younger adversary, "how can you be so cruel?"

"It keeps me going," I said with a smile. "Now would someone be so kind as to refill my coffee?"

With that, they bolted from the kitchen faster than you can say *despair.*

It wasn't that long ago that I'd wished their

summer vacation would last longer. But their recent behavior changed all of that. I wasn't sure if my patience was getting thinner, or if by some strange twist of fate, perhaps the kids truly had gone from bad to intolerable.

Either way, the first day of school could not have come soon enough.

"Time to get up, my little cherub," I whispered into my son's ear on that blessed and joyous first morning of school. "Great things await you."

He opened one fuzzy eye and looked at me. "You're messing with me, right?"

"No Honey. As fate would have it, school starts today!"

I left him moaning as I moved on to another child.

"How can you say that with that kind of face?" responded the twelve-year-old as I cheerily bid him good day.

"What kind of face?" I asked, trying to mask my happiness.

"You're making a smug face."

"I don't even have 'smug' in my face repertoire."

"It's a smug face."

"Mommy is here for you son. Just remember that."

"Yeah," he responded before he rolled over, "so is the militia."

Later that day, my husband and I sat alone and enjoyed a quiet lunch for the first time in over three months. In fact, the silence engulfed us.

"Anything exciting happen today?" He asked me.

"Yeah!" I responded enthusiastically, "I can hear the voices inside my head again."

"Really, and what are they saying?"

"They're saying, 'Hallelujah for education!'"

20

IT'S SO EASY THAT I CAN'T STINKING BELIEVE IT!

    I was honest about my mathematical shortcomings with my husband from the start. I made no bones about telling him that while I could type, multitask, and whip up a heck of a pot roast, any and all calculations and computations would be his and his alone to tackle.
    He seemed to accept it at first. He just smiled at me sweetly, put the financial reports on his side of the desk, and kept the subscription to the *Wall Street Journal* in his name alone.
    Then one night when we were out to dinner, he asked me how much he should tip the waitress. I thought for a moment, then by some fluke of nature I blurted out the 15% calculation like a protégé.
    Naturally, he took it as a sign that I was brilliant and worthy of advanced calculus. Within the week he had me balancing the checkbook, analyzing the stock market, and exploring new avenues for financial diversification.
    "But, Honey," I protested through tears, "you know that I'm not mathematical. I have a hard time figuring my age."
    "Anyone can learn," he responded as he handed me the *Self-Help Guide* by "The New and Friendlier IRS," along with a 41-button calculator and a stack of tax forms three inches thick.
    "You're independent and smart, and now you can be in charge of all of our book work." He sounded like a dang motivational speaker for a late night infomercial. "Now, here are the debits, here are the

credits, and here's a spreadsheet to make your data entries a snap. Why, it's so easy I can't believe it."

A little bit of flattery and suddenly I was in charge of business accounting and our home finances whether I wanted to be or not.

The next time I was swindled by that man, it involved the lawn mower and a hedge trimmer. "But I thought we had a solid understanding," I whined as I stood in the front yard. "I thought we decided I would take care of the inside and you would do the outside."

"Well," my beloved spouse replied, "I was thinking—a little outside work is always good for the soul."

"But my soul is fine indoors. I don't like the heat unless it involves a swimming pool, sun screen, and perhaps a drink with a cute little umbrella."

"But no one looks as pretty out of doors as you do," he said, once again winning me over with flattery.

"Do you mean it?" I replied, blushing like a schoolgirl.

"I do mean it," he said, feigning romance, "and it's so easy you won't believe it. Now come on over here and give this starter rope a pull."

Before I knew it, I was in charge of mowing, sowing, and longing for greener pastures.

I put my foot down when it came to helping him in his line of work. As soon as he started talking to me in terms of lumber and dirt work, I knew that the construction site was not for me and he gave my wishes the utmost respect. Right up until the moment that he desperately needed someone to drive his dump truck.

"But it's a small dump truck," he said of the oversized vehicle that sat on the driveway.

"I won't drive it and you can't make me."

"I just need a bucket and a half of fill sand."

"Do I look like dump truck material to you? My hands are soft, my muscles are flabby, and I don't look good in flannel."

"That dump truck may seem intimidating," he continued as he ignored my protest, "but it drives like a Cadillac. She's got a 5.9 Cummins diesel engine, and with her short box equipped with power take off, you'll be the talk of the town. Besides, you'll look great driving it."

Within the hour I found myself smack dab in the middle of a sand pit as I got my back box filled to the brim by an enormous loader. I sat in the cab with my eyes shut, shaking like a leaf as I clutched my purse and rued the day.

"That's it!" I said sternly when he came home for dinner. I won't be cajoled into doing another thing. I'll file the taxes, I'll mow the lawn, but I won't be your dump truck gal. I absolutely refuse to become any more involved with your line of work."

"No more dump trucks?" he asked as if I'd just hurt his feelings.

"No more dump trucks," I replied roughly.

"How about helping out a little on the job—you can bring us 2 x 4s?"

"I want nothing more to do with the job, the dump trucks, or your 2 x 4s."

"But they're so easy to carry that you won't believe it. Besides, I always love the way the sun shines on your hair when you're carrying lumber."

I think he meant it, too. After all, I have been using a different shampoo.

21

RAISING RALPHIE

Ever notice how boys tend to be magnets for more boys. It's as if they have a homing device that attracts boys for miles around.

There have been times when kids have shown up and stayed for so long that I forgot which boys were actually mine. I've passed out advice and hugs, fixed bruises and cuts, and have been known to ground someone else's child for a week or more.

Take for instance my nephew, Ralphie. Ralphie stopped by for lunch last July and never went back home. He bonded with the family, blended into the background, and fought with our kids so much, we began to think of him as our own.

We really didn't mind having Ralphie around since he was the first kid we'd ever encountered who seemed to like helping out. He would take out the garbage, sweep the floors, and shuck the corn—and all without complaint.

I should have known it was a ruse. There has to be something wrong with a kid who doesn't throw himself into a heap at the prospect of having to pick up his own dirty socks.

It's sort of like having all of the wheels on the shopping cart spin the same way on the same day as the alarm clock goes off at the right time and the kids wake up happy. It's just not normal.

"Ralphie, Honey," I asked him one day just for fun, "would you please clean the bathrooms?" I expected to hear, "But I did it yesterday." or "Why do I always have to?" or the best cop out of all, "You love him more!"

Instead he replied with, "Okay!" And he didn't just say "okay," he said it as if I had just told him that we were heading out to get ice cream cones. I wasn't sure if I could ever get used to a child like that.

As if his eagerness to help weren't enough, his compliments were right on cue. With courtesy as his name and admiration as his game, Ralphie passed out the flattery like the lunch lady on gravy day. "You look lovely today, Aunt Lori," he said with ingratiating politeness one day after school. "The specks of chocolate on your blouse really bring out the blue in your eyes."

"Do you really think so, Ralphie?"

"Oh, I know it to be true. Isn't there something that I could do, that in some small way would lighten your load? Perhaps if I were to mow the yard or to tidy our living space?"

His tactics made our brood look pitiful and I actually bought into it—for awhile. I believed him when he said he was concerned that some of the children weren't buckled up properly. I overlooked the peanut butter on his face when he told me that the other kids had been snacking before supper. When a brawl broke out in the middle of the hallway, it was Ralphie who arose from the chaos and said, "We boys have been fighting, but I feel the situation has been resolved. I only hope we can all learn from this."

I ask you, what mother wouldn't have melted right then and there?

Then one day a piercing scream broke the silence. "What is it?" I asked as I ran into the living room.

"Ralphie just pinched me."

I turned to Ralphie with disbelief. "Ralphie, you didn't just pinch him, did you?"

"I'm only looking out for his best interest," Ralphie said with all of the sincerity he could muster. "He's been watching too much TV and I've become concerned about the violence. It may have a negative impact on his young mind. Therefore, I reached for the remote and I may have accidentally pinched him on the leg. Still, it's a small price to pay for innocence, don't you think?"

I just stood there, blinking. How could I argue with that sort of logic? It was then that it dawned on me that Ralphie was a modern day version of Eddie Haskell and that I, Lori A. Clinch, was taking on the role of none other than June Cleaver.

Heaven help me.

"Well," I finally responded, "you boys play nice and stop fighting. I'm going to go into the kitchen and make cookies."

"Oh, we fully intend to, Aunt Lori. You must teach me your methods of parenting so that I may use them on my own kids someday."

I guess if Ralphie is going to continue hanging around, then it's only going to be a matter of time before I have to don an apron, white gloves, and a pill box hat.

Meanwhile, I'd better turn off the boys' homing device. Larry Mondello could show up any minute.

22

OFFSIDES, ON THE OFFENSE

At the risk of being shunned by my entire family, I must say that I fail to see the importance of football.

Perhaps it is because I don't understand it and am the only individual in my house who thinks an offensive pass interference describes a bad date that gets interrupted by dear old dad.

Generally speaking, I can't follow the path of the ball once the play goes into action—much less decipher what the next guy does with it, or what infractions occur as attempts are made to give it to someone else.

Believe it or not, I never gave the game much thought before I met and married my beloved spouse. Until then, sports were just something that the men did while the women shopped.

My first and full experience with football was on a weekend when my husband promised me romance and then whisked me away to enjoy the Nebraska Cornhuskers. As we sat there in the nosebleed section, I wondered to myself when the endearment was going to kick in and if he had secretly hired a five-string-quartet to appear at our side so he might serenade me.

"How's about a couple of pointers?" I shouted out to him above the roar of the crowd as soon as I realized this was not the case.

"What do you mean?" he asked, not taking his eyes off of the game.

"Like, what's the point of this competition?"

With a disgusted look, he slowly turned my way, shoveled some popcorn into his mouth, and rolled his eyes. Then he said, "The object of the game is to gain possession of the ball and advance it in running or passing plays across the opponent's goal line, or kick it through the air between the opponent's goal posts."

"How brutal!"

"Lori, the goal posts are those tall white sticks at the end of the playing field." Then he rolled his eyes, shoved some more popcorn into his mouth, and turned his attention back to the field.

"Oh! Right. I gotcha. So, do you want to kiss me now?"

"C'mon defense!" he shouted out to the players as if they were listening. "Get your heads in the game!" Then he handed me the popcorn, patted me on the back, and that, my dear friends, was the extent of romance for the day.

I vowed then and there that would be the end of football viewing for me. But that was before the Good Lord, in all of his infinite wisdom, blessed us with boys. Boys who, for reasons I may never understand, love playing football more than eating.

I watch them play it five days a week and twice on Tuesdays—along with a whole bunch of seemingly normal people who think that football is entertaining, exhilarating, and easy to understand. These people know the plays, they know the penalties, and they understand everything with complete knowledge of the play by play action.

Thinking it might be easier to join them than to try and beat them, I decided I should try and learn something about the game. I sat down next to one of the kids last week and asked him a few questions. But he didn't respond so much as throw a few football terms at me and shout out phrases as if he were a sports announcer.

I then decided to ask my friend, Bob. Bob rolled his eyes for a minute before he babbled on about gridirons and encroachments. By the time he got to squib kicks and substitutions, I was longing for a Tylenol and a turnover.

"It's like this," my eye doctor explained as he examined my retinas, "if there's a flag thrown at the snap it's either an off sides, or an illegal motion. The line of scrimmage is where all of the action occurs, and an Intentional Grounding isn't a punishment doled out by well-meaning parents—as one might be inclined to believe—it's a penalty with repercussions. Do you got it?"

"I've got it!" I exclaimed as I walked out the door. I didn't have the heart to tell him that he lost me at *scrimmage*.

I suppose I've no choice but to attend these ball games and remain blissfully ignorant. I shall continue to cheer at the wrong times. I'll shout out "c'mon defense" when it's painfully obvious to everyone else that our team is on the offense. And I shall build on my reputation as, "That wacky gal who—on more than one occasion—starts the wave when the other team scores."

At a recent game, a man, who may or may not be a friend of the family, climbed the bleachers towards me and shouted out, "Hey Lori! They just called a penalty. Any idea what it was?"

"Yes!" I exclaimed, using my best official's tone, "*Traveling*, on the defense, repeat 3rd down."

"But Lori, this is football!"

"Oh yeah, you're right. Then let's repeat the fourth down shall we? And while we're at it, let's kick the ball between the opponent's goal posts."

23

THE DREADED TEENAGE PARTY

It was not long ago that our teenage son expressed a desire to host a gathering in our back garage for a group of his peers. While I felt the color drain from my cheeks, my husband smiled, nodded, and simply said, "That sounds like fun."

I'm sure he was imagining children playing a rousing game of Monopoly with an ice cold glass of Coca Cola. I, on the other hand, had visions of Animal House running through my head.

A teenage party not only takes guts for parents to host it takes forethought, concise planning, and enough common sense to know better.

I consulted our *Handbook for Expert Parenting*. Then I called my parents, friends, and 1-800-dial-a-prayer.

I sat our son down and outlined my expectations with great detail. "There'll be no signs of affection," I said firmly. "No one gets to go knocking on the neighbor's doors, there'll be no explosives of any kind, and under no circumstances is anyone allowed to play hide and go seek."

"What's wrong with hide and go seek?" asked my husband innocently.

"I'm not sure," I replied after a moment's reflection, "but Mary Mimford says it's a bad idea."

"Mary Mimford hasn't had a good time in all of her 48 years. She kills fun wherever she goes. Word on the street is that they once banned her from Disneyland for bumming out Mickey. The woman is like the Gestapo."

I took Mary's advice and placed a plethora of educational magazines about the room. I rented videos from the Discovery channel and dispersed enough religious décor to keep the little devils on the right track.

Then, with all of the ignorance and optimism that a parent such as myself could muster, I held my head up, gave myself a proverbial high five, and went straight to the kitchen for a stiff cup of coffee.

I let fifteen minutes pass before I decided it was time to venture out to check the party. "You're not going to embarrass him are you?" My husband asked as I pulled on fatigues and a ski mask.

"He'll never know I'm there."

"But you look as if you're preparing to run through the thickets."

"Care to join me?"

"No thanks," he replied. "A new episode of 'Engineering Marvels' is coming on and I don't want to miss it."

I gave him a brief lecture entitled, *He's Your Son, Too*, then I slipped out the back door as quietly as possible. I crept across the yard slowly and took extra caution to peek around each tree before I tiptoed to the next. I crawled through the grass, slithered along the walk, and shimmied up to the window. I was just about to look inside when the back screen door shut with a bang. Bright lights went on all over the yard

"*What the heck are you doing?*" I whispered loudly as I spotted my husband on the patio.

"Well," he shouted as if he were hoping his voice would reach me across the Great Divide, "I thought we were going out to check on the kids."

"Why, in the name of all that is intelligent, would you turn on the big lights?"

"Well, I can't just go prancing about in the

dark! You don't want me to break my neck, do you?"

"You can't just turn on the flood lights and sound the sirens," I said with despair. "They'll know we're coming."

DUH!

As far as I was concerned, he might as well have hired a marching band, phoned in the coast guard, and obtained a blow horn to loudly announce, "MAY I HAVE YOUR ATTENTION PLEASE! A PARENT IS APPROACHING THE PREMISES. STASH ALL ILLEGAL ITEMS, CEASE ALL IMMORAL ACTIVITIES, and GOVERN YOURSELVES ACCORDINGLY. REPEAT A PARENT IS APPROACHING THE PREMISES."

"If you announce you're coming," I said as I walked briskly back towards my husband, "all you're going to catch the kids doing is holding hands as they pray the rosary."

The next time we host a teenage assemblage, I'm going to be better prepared. Not only will I don my fatigues, and consult my handbooks, but I'm going to reject my husband's assistance and call in Mary Mimford.

And there's not a jury in the world that would convict me.

24

IN SEARCH OF THE ISOMER

I swear there's nothing as mentally stimulating as a rousing bout of homework with the children. And the older the kids get, the more rousing it becomes.

There's something about predicates, common denominators, and photosynthesis that makes my thinking centers shut down from the overload.

Take the other night for instance. Our fifth grader had my husband detained in the kitchen studying cultures of foreign civilizations and regions so distant that it'd take a plane, a train, and a loaded down donkey to find them.

Meanwhile, I had two fifteen-year-olds marveling at the wonders of science in the living room. They were engaged in a conversation so complex, that I thought it better to hide out in the laundry room and busy myself with things as intricate as lint discovery and sock mating. It's not that I don't want to be an involved parent, but I've already forgotten more about science than I ever needed to know.

I did a bang up job at remaining uninvolved with their studies for a while. Then my eldest offspring, Vernon, shouted, "Hey Mom! Do you have any idea what a monosaccharide is?"

"Of course," I said as I leaned into the room, folding a dishcloth, "I take pride knowing these things. Mono means single item and saccharide is that bad tasting sugar substitute."

"What about polysaccharide?"

"Well, Polly is that cute gal up the street that met and married Huey Saccharide. They have two children and a bird named Splendora."

"This is serious, Mom. It's a big test."

"I know what a polysaccharide is!" said my fifteen-year-old nephew, Ralphie, "It's dehydration synthesis."

It sounded good to me.

"Polysaccharides have nothing to do with dehydration synthesis, Ralphie," said Vernon.

"Yeah-huh," said Ralphie. "Besides, how would you know? You're still looking for the definition of phospholipids."

Just listening to them talk had me longing for the good old days of flash cards and three-letter words. "C'mon, Aunt Lori," Ralphie pleaded, "you have to help us or we are going to bomb this one bad."

"All right," I said with a sigh. "I'll quiz you once. Then I have to get back to my socks. I have a life too, ya know."

I took their book from them and opened it. It's not that *The Protein and Other Molecular Studies For Dummies* wasn't as enticing as it was informative, but if one must know about hydrolysis chemical reactions to function in today's society, I'm in a world of hurt.

"Okay," I started, "what, if anything, can you boys tell me about an isomer?"

"I'm going to let you take that question, Ralphie," said Vernon.

"Well," Ralphie replied, "I'm thinking this is another time where dehydration synthesis properly presents itself."

"You can't just keep saying dehydration synthesis just because it sounds good," Vernon argued.

"How about denaturation then?" said Ralphie.

"You can't just keep spitting out big words."

"He had me fooled," I interjected.

"Mom! He's making me dumber!"

"All right," I said. "I'll tell you boys the definition, but you must memorize this as I go." Then I tried to read the answer without stumbling over the big words, "Isomers are organic compounds with the same molecular formula but different structures and, therefore, (and I paused here for emphasis) different properties."

Vernon and Ralphie looked at me for a minute, then they looked at each other before they looked back at me with astonishment and asked, "Who makes these things up?"

Quite frankly, the definition had me wanting to go and sit in a corner and hum. But as a mother I felt it was my job to do my best to help them understand. "I know, hows about you kids think of isomers as Isotoner gloves. They're both gloves, but they're worn on different hands and they can each hold a different organic property and hang out with the molecules all day if they want to." Personally, I thought it was brilliance at its best. "So, what do you boys think?"

"Mother," said Vernon, "I'm thinking that you're putting more than crème in your coffee."

So much for appreciation of an attempt at brilliance. We spent the better part of thirty minutes reviewing the structure of plant cells and the function of molecules. I'm not sure if I'll retain any knowledge from the night or not. But should anyone ask me if I know why plant cell respirations are conducive, I think dehydration synthesis sounds like a pretty good answer.

25

SPEECH FOR ALL SEASONS: THERE'S NOTHING TO EAT AROUND HERE!

    I happened upon my husband last week as he was looking into the refrigerator with a despondent face. "What are you doing?" I asked.
    "I was wondering what's for supper," he replied. "There's never anything to eat around here."
    "Don't blame me," I retorted. "Check out your fat and sassy children who are sprawled out all over the living room." I peered over his shoulder as he stepped around the corner to take a look. The eldest was studying with a book in his hand and a bag of chips on his lap. Our nephew, Ralphie, was enjoying a bowl of pudding while he watched *Fear Factor*, and the youngest child was seated Indian style on the floor. His eyes were shut, his head was thrown back, and his mouth was open wide as he filled it—straight from the nozzle—with a can of cheese whiz.
    "Are there no limits as to how much they will eat?" Pat asked me.
    "There may be. But if there are, I've yet to find them."
    It's certainly not for a lack of trying. I've used many clever tactics to keep the kids out of the food. I've been known to stash the Cheese Nips in the garage. I've hidden cookies in my sock drawer, beef sticks in the filing cabinet, and concealed the elbow macaroni on the bookshelves, right behind *The Biological Guide For the Curious Mind*.
    But I've come to the conclusion that hiding the goods from the kids is like keeping a fugitive from a bloodhound. It's not possible to win a battle where

these kinds of instincts are involved. It's as if a predator is buried deep in their subconscious and becomes a force to be reckoned with. Why, just last week the kids treed a pizza.

The fact that I go to the store regularly doesn't help at all. Replenish though I may, we're always out of groceries. Take yesterday for instance. I went to the market in anticipation of buying enough supplies to get us through the end of the month. I purchased economy-sized packages for everything from shredded cheese to canned nectarines. I bought Vermicelli in bulk, yams by the dozen, and enough ice cream sandwiches to keep the kids smiling for a month (including a box of low carb ice cream bars as an extra treat for myself.)

I gave my usual "honk for help," as I pulled into the garage. Then I hauled in four gallons of milk, twelve loaves of bread, and an economy-sized bag of apples.

Within minutes, the kids descended upon me like a pack of hungry mongrels. "What did ya get?" one of them asked. "Did you remember to buy pickles?" asked another. "I hope you didn't forget the Velveeta this time. You always forget the Velveeta."

My twelve-year-old son dumped a bag of food onto the kitchen counter and spread out all of the necessary ingredients for a Subway extravaganza. Armed with olives, salami, and pickled peppers, he made a sandwich that would have had Dagwood salivating like a dog.

Ralphie moved past the sandwich buffet and went straight to a session with Frito Lay. He pulled a mixing bowl out of the cupboard and filled it with corn chips faster than you can say, "Macho Nachos." He piled on the guacamole, tossed in a jar of salsa, and finished it off with a huge dollop of sour cream. He could have starred in his own cooking show entitled, *Ralphie Cooks Up For Acapulco*.

The kids consumed and indulged, feasted and devoured. Within minutes they had gobbled down the cereals, devoured the crackers, and had exhausted most of the supplies I had planned for meals for the rest of the week.

By the time they were done, all that was left was a sprig of asparagus and a can of shoepeg corn.

I was hoping my Low Carb Ice Cream bars had survived the onslaught, when Little Charlie walked around the corner gnawing on one and inquired, "How do you eat these things?"

At the end of his workday, my poor and tired husband returned home and once again inquired, "What's for supper?"

"I don't know," I replied as I tripped over an empty can of green beans. "Surprise me."

26

HOUSEKEEPING AND THE CHAOS THEORY

I'm convinced that there are two types of women in this world. There are the orderly and systematic types and there are the chaotic women—such as myself—who cram stuff wherever we can.

The systematic gals make organization look easy. They know where the mate is to each and every sock in their care. They keep their linens in chronological order, alphabetize their canned goods, and have never—for any reason—misplaced a light bulb.

The systematic gals have dust free homes, their desks are without clutter, and the prospect of soggy vegetables in their crisper is more than they can bear.

I am the queen of the chaotic group. While I strive for an organized existence, it eludes me at every turn. My shoes stray from their mates, my best forks hide out in the kids' toy boxes, and I have been searching—for no less than two years—for my spare set of car keys.

While I would love to open a drawer and admire its theme, I can't seem to decide whether the drawer to the right of the sink should be called the 'Haven for Plastic Wrap', or the 'Cozy Corner for Cloves'.

Despite the fact that no one in this house has had a need for a bobby pin in over 36 years, we house one in every drawer—along with a rubber band, one bread tie, and one not-quite-used Q-Tips swab.

Amidst this chaos, there's nothing that I dread more than when my beloved misplaces something. It compares only to being served a search warrant by a band of overzealous FBI agents right before they toss the house. There's no end to where this man will look.

Take January of 2001, for instance. It shall forever be known as "The Winter That I Misplaced the Checkbook."

It started with an inquiry as simple as, "Hey, have you seen the checkbook?" But it quickly evolved into something much more.

Right after we looked in the normal places such as the sewing box and the pocket of my green housecoat, my beloved spouse went through a transformation. He evolved into a man on a mission as he searched through my nightstand and rummaged my magazine racks.

He emptied the laundry hamper, tossed out my coupon box, and then chastised me for my lack of organization in the medicine cabinets. He sorted the contents on my desk, dumped my sock drawer, and had the nerve to search through the boxes of cherished items that I had stashed behind the sofa. (He deemed <u>them</u> trash.)

He messed up the whole house while I ran behind him pleading, "Please stop looking. I'll find it for you. Don't open that door! Don't open that one either! Will you stop opening stuff? Are you insane?" I followed up with my personal favorite, "Why in the world would you check the freezer? And yes! I do have plans for those chicken gizzards!"

The fact that the checkbook turned up behind the potatoes in the drawer under the stove, would make no sense at all to the unseasoned mind. But as any woman worth her salt will tell you, valuable items should always be stashed in the last place that the average thief would think to look.

That's my story, and I'm sticking to it.

Last Saturday night, I walked into our bedroom and caught a glimpse of my husband's feet as they protruded out from under the bed. I instantly knew he'd misplaced something and that a lecture on organization would be sure to follow. "What on earth are you doing under there?" I asked with fear.

"I'm marveling at the mess."

"What are you looking for?"

"I've lost the mate to my black oxfords. Why can't we do something about this clutter?"

"Because it's tiring, it's tedious, and quite frankly, I feel it's beneath us. Besides, why would you think that your Oxfords would be under the bed?"

"Because, I already looked under "O" on the shoe rack and came up empty," he replied sarcastically.

His shoe finally turned up beneath the couch cushion. But not before he rummaged my junk drawers, my glove box, and the cupboard above the refrigerator where I keep the outdated aspirin.

"We're going to have to find a way to organize this mess before we go out of our minds," he said as he tied up his laces.

"Oh, I am so on that!" I replied. "With categorize as my name and regulation as my game, I am going to put organization right at the top of my 'to do' list!"

And I will, too—just as soon as I find my list and a writing utensil.

27

WEIGH-IN ADDS INSULT TO INJURY

My good friends advised me a few years ago to enjoy my thirties while they lasted. "Once you reach forty," they cautioned me, "your body will fall apart, your hair will thin, and you won't be able to read a menu unless your husband is holding it from across the room."

I ignored their warnings and embraced the forties like a ray of sunshine. I squared my shoulders, held my head high, and smiled in the face of adversity.

The first three months of my forties were nothing but smooth sailing. Despite the warnings of my dear friends, I kept my smile intact, my hair follicles held their own, and I could still read the newspaper at arm's length. I didn't skip a beat.

Until last Thursday, that is.

It would have been all together different if I'd injured myself by doing the dew with a bunch of adrenaline junkies. But sadly enough, the biggest thrill I get these days is finding a quarter in the lint trap.

Turns out that a gal my age can pull her spine out of whack by making a simple move. To the tune of *The Old Gray Mare, She Ain't What She Used To Be*, I leaned into the Suburban to retrieve a jacket and found that attempting such a maneuver after forty can have some serious repercussions.

Next thing I knew I was in the doctor's office begging for relief. I sat amidst my fellow patients and a stack of *Golf Digest* magazines, hating every minute.

I tried to look as comfortable as possible, but it wasn't easy. I did find that if I leaned to the left, cocked my head a little, and slightly raised the toe on my right foot, the pain was almost tolerable.

I sat there like a pretzel and scowled as I thought about how I despised the place. Although the doctor is competent and the staff is pleasant, I knew they were going to force me onto their scales and tell me that I weigh ten pounds more than I actually do.

I'm pretty sure that I could walk in there with a bean in my ear, in hopes of a simple bean-ectomy and they'd still ask me to jump up on the scale. "Just hop right up here, Lori. We'll weigh you and *then* the doctor will see about your bean."

When the nurse finally called my name, it was more difficult to stand at attention than I had originally thought. The spirit was willing but the body wouldn't move. I prayed that men in white jackets would come to carry me away. I longed for an over ambitious intern to rush into the room with a gurney and say, "I've got this one, Dr. Carter! She'll be in good hands."

Yet I was left to stand on my own, for no sooner had the nurse called my name than she was gone again—leaving me to upright myself while the other patients looked on. While I would have appreciated some assistance or perhaps a good pull, it would seem that young Ms. Nightingale had sprinted back to the weigh station.

With all the grace and ease of Quasimodo, the great tower dweller of Notre Dame, I finally caught up to my nurse and asked her, "Why the heck do you need to know how much I weigh when I'm in here for back pain?"

"It's procedure, Lori. Same as last time."
"How about if I just give you an approximation and

you can write it down?"

She stared at me with disgust for second before she responded with, "We strive for accuracy."

"The thing is, I already weighed myself this morning," I argued, "and I hear that weighing oneself more than once a day can become addictive."

She pointed at her scale with her pen and said, "Just climb on up here, Honey. It's quite painless."

I continued to protest as I crawled up on the scale. "Tell you what, how's about we just go with the figure my scale gave me this morning. You see, my scale and I have an understanding. It tells me a number that I like, and I don't kick it back into the closet. And just this morning it weighed me in at one-twenty……wait! I don't weigh that much! You aren't going to chart that weight, are you?"

"Hmm, hmm," she replied with a quick click of her pen.

"Well then, I think you should also chart that I had a hefty bagel for breakfast this morning and a large coffee. We need to take into account that I'm wearing winter garments and a pair of chunky shoes that I would have removed if I could bend over."

When the doctor entered the room a few minutes later he asked me, "So Lori, what are you here for today?"

"Old age, a bum back, and now that Nurse Reality shed the light on my obesity, I'll be needing some medication for depression."

28

PARENTING ADVICE FROM DR. HASNOKIDS

I was going through an old stack of magazines the other day when I ran across one called, *Modern Day Moms*. It was a periodical with a fine collection of wisdom and tact for parents who are struggling with the task of child rearing.

I leafed through articles regarding home remedies, stress-proof bedtimes, and the no-panic guide to kids' cooties.

Suddenly an article entitled; "Are You a Screamer?" jumped out at me like a spook.

"Do you holler at your kids until your voice cracks?" it asked of me. "Does your family think you're a shrew? Do your neighbors insist that you keep your windows closed on nice days to promote peace in the community?"

I fidgeted for a minute as the guilt washed over me. Heaven knows I wouldn't scream if it weren't necessary. After all, as any seasoned parent will tell you, mental telepathy is not an effective mode of communication.

The kind folks at *Modern Day Moms* deemed screaming a bad thing. They even quoted Dr. C.I. Hasnokids, from the Institute for Better Ancestry, who feels that discipline is more practical when delivered with a hushed tone. For example, rather than shrieking at the child who just broke your great-grandmother's sandwich plate, one could say, "Billy, I am very disappointed that you used your father's sledge hammer on this priceless family heirloom. Tell me, Honey, what better choices could you have made?"

Heaven knows I wouldn't want to raise mentally scarred children. So I decided then and there to give this system of modern day parenting a go.

It worked like a dream while the kids were in school. And during the sleeping hours, I was the best mother on the planet. In fact, things went splendidly for almost a day—until I happened upon the little cherubs in what was once a clean kitchen.

What had previously sparkled and shone, was now wall to wall cereal. Abandoned shoes and socks were strewn about, athletic devices littered the floor, and I swear there was a misty-green fog that hung low in the air.

I darest say that even Carol Brady, the great soft spoken mother of all times, would have roared at the situation—and she had a housekeeper.

Still, I'd made myself a promise and I intended to follow through. I put my plan into action and asked them—in my new soft voice—to collect their belongings and stow them in their proper places. Sadly enough, I received no reaction.

Next—as Dr. Hasnokids advised—I spoke sternly and in a no-nonsense tone. I even pointed my finger for emphasis.

No one so much as looked my way. Suddenly, all that I'd strived for went out the window. I planted my feet, filled my lungs and threw my head back as I screamed to the heavens, "If you kids know what's good for you, you'll get this mess cleaned up right now. And I mean it!"

The walls vibrated, the windows rattled, and my little charges jumped into action.

Although I'll most likely remain a screamer, I thought I could work on raising children who felt loved—as was clearly outlined on page 197 of *Modern Day Mothering*.

"Huey," I said to my twelve-year-old during the very next crisis, "you may not beat your brother's brow with a Tonka truck. Now come in here and we'll make a chart and Mommy will give you a sticker for each positive choice that you make."

"Yeah," replied Huey, as he turned to his younger brother. "And if I make five good choices in a row, Mom's going to replace you with a puppy."

I clearly recalled page 146 saying, "Analyze. Get into your child's head. Stoop to his level. Become one with his mind so that you can perceive and understand." Yesterday, the opportunity for perception presented itself with flying colors. Little Charlie came into the room and screamed out that his older brother had not only taken his favorite wristband, but had called him a crybaby in the process.

If there were ever a place where positive parenting would get a chance to work its magic, it would be here. "And tell me, young Charlie," I responded with sincerity, "how did that make you feel?"

"What do you mean—'how does that make me feel?' He's an idiot!"

"That's a good place to start, Honey. Let your emotions out. Tell it the way it is."

With that, young Charlie stopped and looked at me as if I were an alien. He blinked a couple of times, shook his head and walked away.

I gotta hand it to the folks at *Modern Day Mothering*. They really know how to give a gal the peace she strives for.

29

WHEN IN DOUBT, BLAME THE RECEPTION

I was three forks into a salad the other day when I received the interruption a mother dislikes most—The Dreaded Cell Phone Call. It rang out loud and clear, bringing stares from those around me. I rummaged through my purse as I cursed technology and answered to static with a hushed, "Hello."

Although I could barely make out what was being said, the voice on the other end was clearly one of my own children. It sounded as though he were standing in a wind tunnel in Siberia and talking through a cone.

"Hello!" I said again. A woman with intellect would have simply hung up, threw caution to the wind, and returned to her lettuce.

But not me. You can blame it on curiosity. Blame it on a sense of responsibility. Blame it on a woman who doesn't have the sense God gave a goat. But, heaven help me, I needed to hear what he had to say.

I stood up at the table and put my index finger in my right ear. I then looked down, tilted my head to the right and leaned to the left. I also found that if I shut my right eye, I could almost make out my son's voice at the other end.

"Mom, Mom, can you hear me?"

"Yes," I whispered, as I looked around at the inquisitive eyes and tried not to move for fear of losing reception.

He said a few more words, mumbled something that sounded like *gesundheit,* and then the line went dead. Leaving me in a room full in inquiring minds with nothing left to do but to go back to my salad and hope that he called back.

Or not.

Way back in my pre-cell phone days, I roamed in peace. I shopped until I dropped, ran errands uninterrupted, and whiled away the hours at social functions in the blissful ignorance of being unreachable.

Then, in a moment of stupidity, I campaigned for a cell phone like a lobbyist on Capitol Hill. I presented with facts and statistics so compelling that even my husband—the great tightwad of his time—could not dispute them.

"Analyze this, Honey," I said as I pointed to a chart with my laser pen, "I'll always be a phone call away, the family will never be without my expertise, and the kids will be able to contact me at a moments notice." I made it all sound as if it were a good thing.

Looking back I realize it was a stupid argument coming from a woman who hadn't had a moment to herself in over twelve years.

The other morning, the most ludicrous of all cell phone scenarios transpired. Naturally, it occurred when I was doing my best to impress a group of mere acquaintances. I was mingling as if I had it all under control—pretending as though I hadn't a care.

"My yes," I said with faux confidence as I held my cell phone tight. "Our children are independent of us these days. Why, they tend to themselves without so much as a fleeting thought."

Just then my phone rang out across the great divide. The room went silent, conversation ceased to exist, and everyone looked my way as they waited with bated breath to see what emergency had warranted The Dreaded Cell Phone Call.

"Hello," I whispered into the receiver as I smiled weakly at those around me. I could hear one of the kids screaming into the receiver, yet I couldn't quite make out the words.

"What did you say, Honey?"

"Har-rareumpph (*static*) heremortaphizingpin."

"I can't hear you."

Again, I was left to take the matter of reception into my own hands. I stepped to the left and took a soft dip in the hip. I looked down, kicked off my right shoe, and I closed my right eye.

Just then, something miraculous occurred. It was as if the upper atmosphere shifted. Perhaps the Jet Stream relocated or a butterfly sneezed in South America and caused a low-pressure system to develop over Montana. No matter. The miracle of it was, my cell phone cleared up for the first time in 4 years. Although I was scared to move, I could finally hear every word that my little Huey was saying.

"I said I forgot my science paper," he sang out loud and clear. "I'll need you to bring it to me right away. And oh yeah! You might have to glue some stuff."

With that, I hung up and blamed it on bad reception. After all, the kid didn't have to know that I had my right eye closed.

30

FABIO VS. BOB

My husband has two different personalities. First, there is the romantic side—the Fabio-like personality that enjoys moonlit walks, engaging conversation, and washing the dishes.

Fabio doesn't hang out much—although he did show up from time to time during our courting years—bringing roses, opening doors, and gazing at me lovingly across a candle-lit table.

Now days, I'm lucky to receive a look from above the newspaper. That's where Bob—personality number two—comes in. Instead of telling me how lovely my eyes look as they dance in the kitchen lights, Bob likes to say, "uh-huh," and "I'll take more coffee while you're up."

He never serenades me with love songs, never fills a room with roses, and has never—not once—given me a coupon for a back rub that I could redeem at a moment's notice. He even scoffed at the t-shirt I gave him with my picture on it that said, "My heart belongs to Lori."

Fabio would have worn it.

Recently, we decided to build a home together. That's when Bob all but kicked Fabio's rear end right out the door. He put an end to romance, halted all feelings of endearment, and hung a mental sign across his head that says, "Fabio doesn't live here anymore."

Romance did surface briefly in August, however, when the weather was sultry and the heat intense. He appeared by my side as I stood amongst the construction materials and handed me a diet coke. "Fabio?" I asked as I took the soda. I was overwhelmed with emotion. "Gosh, I hardly know what to think!" I said as I wiped the sweat from my brow and brushed a tumbleweed out of my hair.

He said nothing. He just handed me a hammer and a bucket full of nails and told me to get back to work.

Thanks a lot Bob.

In the past several months I've spent 100 degree days in a dust bowl, long hours in high winds, and learned first hand how to install a foam block foundation. I—the wife of Bob—have cut and measured lumber, glued down plywood, and learned how to run a power trowel. I've become the resident expert on the power screed, run a wacker-packer like no one's business, and if someone should need their dump truck dumped, I'd be the gal.

The other day a child who may or may not have belonged to me, came up to me and gave me a hug. With all the love I could muster, I turned to him and said, "Dang, Honey, you have to go home and shower. YOU seriously SMELL!"

To which the child replied, "Sorry, but that smell belongs to you, Mom."

It's totally ruining my reputation as a girly girl.

Most importantly, I resent wearing construction garb. The hard hat flattens my hair, the goggles leave indentations on my face that won't go away for days, and—I don't mind telling you—the tool belts do not compliment my hips.

Above all, construction boots are heavy to wear and make a make a gal's legs look chunky. I know that open toed shoes are not recommended on the job site, but—in my defense—I know where my toes are at all times. I don't carry skill saws, nor do I lug around anchors and anvils.

I was good to go right up until the moment when my family-of-men dragged a wall across my toe. Not just any wall, mind you, but a genetically engineered and manufactured support with "zig-zag" framing members—and a heavy one at that.

I didn't scream loudly as one might expect, but I did have thoughts of anger as I danced in pain.

As I was in the middle of suppressing curse words and masking my anguish, I caught a glimpse of my family. Bob and all of his boys were just standing there looking at me with disgust. No compassion, mind you, just simple unadulterated distaste.

Not a one of them rushed to my aid. No one offered their condolences, sympathy, or a Band-Aid for that matter.

Nope, they simply looked at me with repulsion. Bob and his band of charges. Finally, Vernon, my eldest and wisecracking child, asked me, "Can you say steel toed work boots?"

Later, as I sat in the chair with my foot elevated, my husband appeared at my side and asked, "Does it hurt much?"

"Like a monkey."

"Perhaps you should stay home tomorrow and just take it easy."

"Do you really think so?"

"Yeah. You could use a break."

I just love it when he's Fabio.

31

THIS HOLE IN THE WALL GANG HANGS PICTURES

When my parents bought a new house, my father forbade my mother from putting any nails into the new and unblemished walls. He even went so far as to hide the nails and remove all of the hammers from the house.

It was quite a restriction for a woman with a decorative flair. She held out for what must have seemed like hours before she tried a new approach.

"For the love of fasteners!" he exclaimed when she walked into the room with a stainless steel meat tenderizer and a tent stake. "Whose heart are you going to drive that spike into?"

"Well," she replied with a smirk, "I thought you wouldn't mind if I created a look of creativity over here in the corner."

"That's not creativity," he shouted as he went pale, "that's a demolition derby."

"Would you prefer it if I suspended this picture from a chain and wore it around my neck? Or better yet, we'll get one of the kids to stand in the corner and hold it up whenever company comes over."

"Oh, give me that thing," he said as he took the picture from her. "I'll have to do it myself if I'm going to keep the walls from looking like a dart board."

Then, as people of his gender are prone to do, he pulled out his do-it-yourselfer guide and quickly turned to chapter 32 entitled, "The Right Procedures for Artistic Attachments." "I'll need my needle nosed pliers, my laser level, and a tape measure to assure us of precise centering," he said as he donned his goggles and a pair of gloves. Then he put on his hard hat, fastened his tool belt, and said, "Now watch and learn. With accuracy and great efficiency I shall utilize my stud finder to sense the dielectric constant and insulating value. Then we can assess the area, and get this procedure underway."

Although my mother and I pretended to listen to his little demonstration with great interest, the only thing that I learned that day was that I should never ever try to hang a picture if there's a man around.

This is especially true if my father-in-law is in the area. The man feels that a nail hole in the wall is borderline criminal and is the biggest nail-hater of his time. Before a picture can be hung, an entire strategy must be implemented. Papers must be filed, phone calls have to be made, and the right people have to come out to inspect probable sites. Above all, never—not once ever—should more than one nail hole occur in any picture hanging location.

Why, he'd shudder to think.

So when I purchased a lovely picture for my dear mother-in-law's birthday, she and I did as women with intellect are prone to do. We waited until that man was out of the house.

"Is the coast clear?" I asked as I crept through the front door.

"We should be good to go for a while," she whispered. "He's having coffee with his nail-hating buddies. Do you have the goods?"

"A bucket of nails and the best meat tenderizing club that money can buy. Where shall I pound the spike?"

"In the bedroom."

"Won't he notice?"

"He may," she replied, "but at his age I can

convince him that things have always been this way and that his mind is slipping."

"How's this look, girl?" I asked as I held the picture up to the wall.

"Move it to the left."

"Here?"

"Nope, that's too far. Go back to the right. Now up. Okay, now down a bit."

"Here?"

"Perfect! Nail it!"

It seemed correct. It really did. Then we stood back for a moment and admired our work—before we pulled the nail back out and re-inserted it three inches over to the right. Then, following another quick viewing, we moved it back an inch and up to the left.

"What have you girls been up to?" my father-in-law asked upon his return.

"Oh, just a little dusting and sprucing the place up a bit," I said as I sipped my coffee.

"That story sounds like it's full of holes to me," he replied.

Boy, he sure hit the nail on the head with that one.

32

THE SNOW DAY: CRUEL AND UNUSUAL

I have to be honest with you when I say I felt totally let down by our school system's superintendent, Bill Diehard. When we enrolled our children into the system under his jurisdiction some eleven years ago, other parents assured us that snow days were never allowed.

For years I've enjoyed saying to the kids, "Oh, there'll be school tomorrow. There's always school tomorrow. Even if Mr. Diehard has to come around on a dog-pulled sled to get you there, school will be in session." Then I'd chuckle as I added, "Trust me."

Since our darling nephew, Ralphie, has recently come to stay, he's not familiar with how Mr. Diehard runs things. He's not accustomed to the fortitude and valor of a man who has been known to keep school in session despite the worst of nature's furies.

Therefore, I spent the better part of our most recent snowstorm yuking it up at his expense. "Now that you're with us, Ralphie, there'll be no more snow days for you, little Mister. We are strong, we are resilient, and we are committed to education even in the face of adversity. Mr. Diehard hasn't called a snow day in over 100 years. He wouldn't do so even to save his very soul."

Imagine my chagrin when my sister phoned the other night. I was in the middle of a prayer of praise—giving thanks to the Man upstairs that the long weekend had ended. I was on my sixth thank-you and grinning like a Cheshire cat, when I heard the kids whoop it up in the kitchen as if Ed McMahon had just rung the doorbell and presented them with a million dollar check.

As I was breathing in relief and counting down the moments to bedtime, my sister was informing the kids that their weekend had been extended by another joyous day.

They arrived in the living room and began doing cartwheels. They did the tunnel walk out of the back hallway, formed a pyramid, and catapulted the youngest into the air. With invisible pom-poms and blow horns made out of my *Better Homes and Gardens* magazines, they exclaimed, "We say 'snow,' you say 'day,' 'snow,' 'day,' 'snow,' 'day!'"

As if that weren't enough, they formed a spirit line and ran in front of the TV with a large sign that said, "MAKE SOME NOISE!"

Talk about rubbing it in.

They concluded their pep rally with one final round of "Stand UP, be proud, state your case, out loud, WE GET A SNOWDAY!" Then they locked their arms, and swayed from side to side as they sang out an off-key rendition of "Let It Snow, Let It Snow, Let It Snow." It was more than I could bear.

My sister laughed until she cried, my parents phoned to chuckle at my expense, and the kids continued to party with such excitement that I considered knock out drops to restore the peace and tranquility that I had coming to me.

"At least you get to sleep in tomorrow," said my little Lawrence as he handed me a hankie. I have to admit, the idea did appeal to me. I could have done it, too, if my husband, (aka Captain Morning) hadn't waked up at the crack of dawn and realized that he was snowed in as well.

His heart must have been filled with joy as he ripped the blankets off of me at six a.m. and hollered loudly, "LoriLoriLori! Are you up for all day? Do you want a cup of coffee? Do you want to look at the snow? Just think, if I'm here and you're here and the kids are all here, we can all spend the entire day together. Right here in the house. Isn't it grand?"

I think I'll load up the dog sled and send for Mr. Diehard. If I'm to be in the midst of all of this sheer excitement, there's no reason on earth he shouldn't be here to share it with me.

33

THE KEY TO ANY TEENAGER'S HEART: $5

Although my children have been known to make me crazy, I kind of like having them around. Suffice it to say I'd never stoop to a level where I'd offer them cash compensation to leave the house. I'm like a referee at a boxing match—they give me a purpose.

Yet, every time my eldest son departs, it costs me upwards of five bucks. We take a hit to the pocketbook whether that kid is going to school, a church function, or a back yard bash up the neighbor's alley.

Although pizza runs a close second, he loves money more than anything. Currency is like oxygen to that child. Waving money in his face is like passing smelling salts under the nose of a dazed boxer. Just the other day, I caught him digging in my wallet. A lesser woman would have spun on her heel and blown a gasket.

"What are you doing?" I shrieked.

"Dad said I could get five bucks." (Isn't that just like a man?)

"And what, pray-tell do you need five bucks for?"

"Some of the guys are getting together at Baxter's tonight for Playstation."

"Why would you need five bucks for that?"

"I have to pay Kramer back for the punches that I used on his lunch tickets."

"But I gave you money for a lunch ticket."

"Yeah, but I gave that money to Lewis."

"Then Lewis should pay you back."

"Well, he would except that I ran up minutes on his cell phone. Lewis has had a cell phone for six months. Why can't I have a cell phone?"

"Because we're still trying to pay off the debt you've owed to Johnson since the third grade." (That's what you get when your kid borrows from a mathematical genius, the interest alone will kill ya.)

"Well, Charlie's cavities cost $250. Since my hygiene is stellar, don't you feel I deserve adequate compensation?"

You have to hand it to the kid—he does have a brilliant mind.

His needing money has become second nature. I've taken to keeping five-dollar bills in my pockets at all times, passing them out like an ATM machine every time he leaves my side.

Recently, however, I experienced one of those joyful parenting moments when it seemed that he genuinely needed me. His team had just finished up with the state championship for the football season. I was standing outside the stadium when he called me on Lewis' cell phone. "Mom?" I heard him ask desperately.

"Yes, Honey," I replied, "where are you?"

"The whole team is outside the locker room and all of the other parents are here."

"All of the parents?" I asked as if I'd just taken a blow to the gut.

He was quiet for a moment and then he responded with, "Everyone that cares."

"Oh my goodness, shall I come and be with you?"

"Gosh, Mom, that'd be really nice," he said, and the last part of his statement rang out in my ears and inflicted guilt upon my very soul.

"I'll be right there!" I exclaimed loudly. I dropped my blanket, my blow horn, and my big fat "number one" blow-up finger and ran like the wind.

"What kind of mother," I asked myself as I pushed through the crowd, "wouldn't be there for her child?"

When I arrived at the locker room, parents swarmed me. "Lori, where have you been?" asked an individual as I passed. "Vernon has been looking for you!" exclaimed another with the proverbial, "*tsk tsk*."

Finally, I could see his sweet face over the mass of people. He was searching for me and I swear I saw a look of desperation in his eyes. "Vernon!" I exclaimed, "I'm over here, Honey. It is I, your mother!"

I pushed my way through until, alas, I was at his side. My heart ached as I threw my arms around him. I was out of breath and weak in the knees. "You needed me, didn't you, Honey? I'm so sorry. I didn't know. But I'm here now and that's all that matters."

"Great," he replied as he smacked me on the back. "I thought you'd never get here. Some of us are going out for pizza."

"Oh, did you want me to come along?"

"Gosh no, Mom!" he practically screamed, indicating that if I dared to show up at any post-game event, he may self-destruct with the humility of it all. "But I'm running a bit thin in the wallet. Could you hit me with a ten-spot?"

34

WHAT THE TOWEL DID THAT KID JUST SAY?

I think the short days of winter are taking their toll on our family. I'm really hoping that the sun will start taking the long trip around the planet again sometime real soon. I'm not so sure that we can take all of the indoor time with all of us for much longer.

That's for stinking sure.

Take tonight for instance. My little Lawrence took a nice, long shower only to discover that there were no clean towels in the bathroom. He shook off as much excess water as he could before he opened the bathroom door and loudly exclaimed, "I need a towel!"

I was rather busy at the time. Turns out someone put a glass inside the garbage disposal and then, for reasons we may never understand, turned it on. A better mother would have done an investigation, called in witnesses, and perhaps summoned a team of experts to get to the bottom of the situation. A more suitable woman would have checked out alibis, interviewed friends, and interrogated suspects until they broke under pressure.

But around here, it was just another incident that involved an appliance and a piece of raw material. A fragment of material that, if not handled properly, could sever a limb and render a mother useless for the better part of a week.

I remained an arm's length into the disposal in an attempt to try and force it to give birth to a huge chunk of glass that simply wouldn't fit back through the hole. Meanwhile, my dear Lawrence was in the bathroom, cold, and screaming for a towel as if it were the end of the earth and he was the last man standing in a wasteland of proverbial nakedness.

I did what any mother in my situation would be prone to do, and passed some of the parental responsibilities on to my eldest child. "Vernon!" I hollered without letting go of the chunk of glass, "get him a towel out of the other bathroom!"

Before I go on, I feel I should mention that good mothers do not curse—especially in front of the children. And I strive to be good. God knows I do. Cursing mothers raise cursing children, so I only curse when I'm really mad. Then, of course, there's the occasional bout in the afternoon when no one's around.

Still, I stand firm. My children are NOT allowed to curse. Not once, not ever. Yet apparently my dear Vernon, in response to my request that he simply go and get a towel out of the bathroom for his brother, yelled—and at the top of his lungs, I might add—"Lawrence, get the HELL out of the bathroom."

Imagine my home when this hits the fan. Ralphie took a deep breath in feigned shock, Little Charlie dropped a noodle out of his mouth and Huey, (our destined-to-be-a-priest child) suddenly appeared at my side to inquire, "Did you know that Vernon just said 'hell'? You are not going to just stand here and allow him to curse are you? Do you want me to call in the response team?"

As I said, I may be an occasional curser, but I still discipline my children for "shut up" and "moron."

I am quite certain that had I actually heard Vernon say hell, I would have blown a gasket. But you see, I was involved with the disposal and doing my darndest to remain composed as I tried to digest the fact that some ignoramus tried to grind up a glass and send it through the city's sanitation system.

I turned to Huey, my destined-to-be-a-priest child, and inquired, "What did you just say?"

"I said Vernon just told Lawrence to get the HELL out of the bathroom."

I sucked in a deep breath and looked at Huey in disbelief, "You did not just say hell!"

"I didn't say hell," he replied. "Vernon said hell."

I knew full good and well that Huey had just said hell. But I wasn't sure if it was OK or not, since he was simply repeating what he thought his older brother had said. I made a mental note to look that up in my *Mother's Guide to Better Parenting* book, and then turned to Vernon.

"Did you say hell?"

"Well," Vernon replied with a smirk, "you're the one that told me to tell him to get the *hell* out of the bathroom."

"I said towel!"

"Oh," he said as he looked at me and blinked. "Well then, that does make a difference now doesn't it?" Then he walked back to the hallway and called out to his poor, wet brother, "Hey Lawrence, Mom said to get the towel out of the bathroom."

I can't help but wonder how all of this will sound when it comes out in therapy.

35

HE WANTS $125 SHOES FOR CHRISTMAS

It's Christmas time. Oh, the unadulterated bliss, with holiday greetings, great happy meetings, and "It's The Most Wonderful Time of the Year" constantly playing on the radio. By the way, did you ever notice that a man sings that song?
Just an observation.
The big day is just around the corner. Yet my shopping isn't done, my cookies aren't baked, and my cards are strewn about the abode as I desperately search for Aunt Bernadeen's new address. Basically my goose is cooked.
If you know what I mean.
Any woman worth her salt is more than likely breaking into a sweat as she tries to think up the perfect gift. She bargain hunts, clips coupons with a frenzy, and has risen at unholy hours for six days running. There are no limits to what a mother will endure for the sake of a good sale.
A lesser woman would simply settle for socket wrench sets and Chia Pets.
But the good mother perseveres so that the children she so dearly loves won't suffer disappointment. It's their smiling faces on Christmas morning that she dreams of, the joy in their hearts, and their never-ending expression of gratitude to the person who made it all possible: that spotlight stealer, Santa Claus.
Still, gift exchanging seems to be on everyone's mind. Even my handsome and loving husband seems to be tossing it around.

"What would you like for Christmas this year?" he asked me as he put a jewelry ad through the shredder. "And let's not forget the new garage doors we just purchased."

Yeah, I can see him on his late, great December 24th purchase now. He'll be scrambling for a gift, only to discover that there's nothing left but rain gauges by Ronco. But I can't think about that right now. I have the kids to worry about. Buying for them becomes more challenging every year. Back in the days of Batman and G.I. Joe, life was simple. I could walk down the isles and say, "wow!" "ooooo" and "oh, my gosh, our little precious just has to have it!"

Nowadays, it's simply, been there, done that. Bought it, hated it, broke it, trashed it, gave it away, and how many batteries can that dang thing go through? I've learned that battery-operated cars don't hold up under pressure—nor do they make the kids into better drivers. Stretch Armstrong cannot double as a bungee cord, and although a flaming tires racing set seems enticing, the long orange plastic tracks are eventually going to become weapons in the hands of a child who knows how to use them.

In a moment of desperation, I gathered the children around in hopes of getting some ideas. Yet, when I pressed them for information, the oldest just shrugged his shoulders, and the youngest asked for a pack of gum.

"Surprise me," said Lawrence, my wise and practical child.

"I don't want to surprise you. I want a list. How about a football?"

"Got one."

"How's your Monopoly set holding up?"

"Our Monopoly set is fine. Besides Bobby Mimford says Monopoly is like an educational game in disguise."

As I sat there with a pen and an empty tablet, I decided that I really don't like Bobby Mimford. I was just about to say so when my Huey blurted out, "Hey, I know what I want!"

"What?" I exclaimed with excitement as I put my pen to my tablet and prepared to write something down.

"T-Mac 4s."

My chest was tightening, and my palms began to sweat as I thought about last year's fiasco with the MP-3, the DVD, and the much-coveted analog controller for the PS-2. Whatever happened to the good old days when you could make a kid happy with a Kidz Bop album and a nice pair of socks?

"T-Mac 4s?" I said, making no attempt to hide my disgust.

"Yeah, T-Mac 4s are like these really cool basketball shoes."

"Basketball shoes?" Now he was talking my language. Shoes are simple. They're practical and should be at the top of everyone's no-nonsense list.

"Yes," he added before I finished writing it down, "And they're only $125."

Gulp.

"A hundred and twenty-five dollars? Are you insane?"

"No, and I want them more than anything. I'd walk 500 miles for those shoes. I'd climb to the tallest mountain top and swim to the depths of the ocean for a pair of T-Mac 4s." Then he leaned toward me, raised an eyebrow, and as cute as a bug he added with an all-knowing smile, "Santa could bring them."

You know, that kid won't think he's so cute when he discovers that spotlight-stealin' Santa has left him nothing more than a socket wrench set by Ronco.

36

HE MAKES DRIVING OFF SOUND SIMPLE

Well, he went ahead and did it. I asked him not to, pleaded in fact. I even offered cash compensation. But he ignored my offers and turned 16 anyway.

I didn't even realize how hard it would be until just the other day when I was forced to think about handing him the keys to my cherished Suburban for the very first time. I was pale as a ghost and shaking like a leaf. My hands were clammy. I could barely catch a breath and I felt weak in the knees. I tried to comfort myself with the fact that he could bring me back a gallon of milk, but nothing seemed to help.

Meanwhile, he was grinning like a cymbal-clanging monkey as he sported his brand new, plastic encased driver's license. He flashed it as if he'd been locked up for years, and was finally handed his ticket to freedom.

"Are you sure you have to go?" I asked him as I clutched my car keys tightly in my fist.

"Yes, Mother," he said slowly and without remorse, "I am *quite* sure."

"How's about a little visit first. We can sit down and re-hash old times."

"I'm only 16. I don't have old times yet."

"Well then," I said, "I can tell you about mine. Did I ever tell you about the time..."

"Mom!" he exclaimed, interrupting my stroll down memory lane, "you can put this off, but you can't change it. Now please release your death grip on the car keys and hand them over."

"But we haven't even had a cookie yet. Don't you want a cookie?"

"We haven't had a cookie in the house for months. I'm going to be late."

"Oh, all right," I replied as I surrendered. "Are you wearing your contacts? You should never drive without corrective eye wear."

"Yes, I'm wearing my contacts."

"What about shoes? There are laws in this state that prohibit driving barefoot."

"I'm wearing shoes."

"You won't forget to buckle up will you? Seat belts save lives ya know."

"Trust me Mom. Mentally, I'm already confined."

"Good. Do you have a cell phone?"

"No, you said it was too expensive."

"Oh, yes, that's right. Okay, here, take my cell phone, and here's my triple A card in case you have an emergency. Do you know where the flashlight is? The jack? The tire iron and the shovel? Have you packed an emergency road side kit including flares and high energy granola bars?"

"For Pete's sake, Mom, I'm not driving through Arctic Tundra. Can I please just go?"

Just go? He made it sound so simple. I thought letting him go to pre-school was hard—knowing he'd be at the mercy of someone who didn't love him as much as I. Against my better judgment, I've let him spend time away from home, play outside after dark, and demonstrate independence while crossing the street. Yet it all paled in comparison to handing him the keys and watching drive away.

Friends had warned me that this day would come. "You're going to have to let him grow up. You know that, don't you?" a woman who may or may not have been a friend said to me over lunch a month ago.

"When he turns the big one-six, you'll have to hand him the keys to your car and watch him spin out of your life."

But it had seemed light years away—something that other parents dealt with, perhaps an older crowd.

I've spent the better part of this past year teaching him the ins and outs of driving. It was harrowing to say the least. He went too fast. He drove too slow. He sped up for a red light and sat through a green one. His corners were square. His in-between-car-ratio was off and I swear he once drove close enough to a '76 Oldsmobile to suck the rust right off its body. How could I possibly trust him to drive without my constant interjections?

"So, Mom, are you going to hand me the keys or not?" he asked, bringing me back to reality. I stood and looked at him for what must have seemed like an eternity. I finally handed him the keys and watched him climb behind the wheel. He turned the key long enough for the starter to make a grinding sound. Then he put it in reverse and backed into the street. Suddenly he slammed on the brakes, shifted into forward with a jolt and let out a big "Woo-hoo!" as he drove out of sight.

Gosh, I thought to myself as I fought back the tears, *I wonder if he'll remember to bring me back a gallon of milk.*

37

A BAD CASE OF THE 'MAN HANDS'

While I have a love for fashion, décor, and the occasional bling bling, my darling husband is mesmerized with building.

I'd just as soon indulge in new hairstyles, clothing lines, and the latest color to paint the walls. His interest is restricted to construction and anything that can be held together with nails. Now that he has decided to build us a new house he's in seventh heaven.

To keep things interesting, he likes to drag me into the process whenever possible. Knowing full good and well that construction and fabrication are not my forte, he ignores my objections and cons me into helping by appealing to my romantic side.

"How about spending some time with me today?" he asked me last week with a wink and a smile.

"Really?" I asked with excitement. "What do you want to do? Go to a movie? Take a stroll in the park? Oh, I know—there's a new cute little shop downtown. Do we dare?"

"No, I was thinking more along the lines of you coming to work on the house with me. I'll bring coffee!"

"I can have coffee anytime," I said with a frown. "Besides, my back still aches from the last time I worked with you. I think I'll just stay home and think up a New Year's resolution."

"You don't need a resolution. Besides, I have a great job for you this time. It's called weatherproofing."

Weatherproofing? Any woman with an ounce of intellect would have run and hid at the prospect. Yet, for reasons we may never understand, I was out of fashionable attire and into old clothes faster than you can say *deranged*.

"Do you know what this is?" he asked as he held up an aerosol can with a straw coming out of the nozzle.

"A new and fun way to spritz my hair?"

"No, this is the way to begin the weatherization process. You just take this can, point the straw and dispense it." It was obvious that he was enjoying his little demo, and although I've suffered from working with him on more that one occasion, spraying yellow stuff around openings did sound simple. He finished up with, "This is so easy I can't believe it." Then he handed me the can and walked away.

I dispensed for quite some time and never realized I was in trouble until I tried to set the can down. Turns out the fun and billowy yellow stuff not only was a crack-filler but had adhesive properties as well.

I was in the middle of the can removal process when I noticed the warning in large red letters on the canister that read: *WEAR PROTECTIVE GLOVES WHEN USING THIS PRODUCT.*

Well, color me informed a day late and a dollar short. Any woman with the sense that God gave a goat would have read the instructions on the can *before* using it. But when my beloved spouse was going through the demonstrative process, he made no mention of protective anything. He simply squirted and said, "It's so easy I can't believe it."

Soap and water did nothing to remove it. Lacquer thinner didn't help and although the gasoline seemed like a good idea at the time, it only made my exposed skin raw.

Holding my hands as if I were wearing yellow foamy mittens, I marched my smelly self around to the back of the house where I found my beloved whistling on the roof.

"How do you get this stinking stuff off?" I screamed up at him.

"What stuff?" he asked, as if he didn't already know.

"This yellow stuff. Look at me. I'm hideous!"

"Oh!" he responded. "You should have put on gloves before using that stuff."

"Duh!" I said as I stomped like a two-year-old. "Do you have chemicals to remove it?"

"Nope!"

"What about a bar of Lava soap and a pumice stone?"

"Nope, nothing will take that stuff off," he yelled down at me before he repeated, "You should have been wearing gloves!"

It was a moment of true ignorance that left me with nothing to show for it but a grimy pair of man-hands. I quickly found myself asking anyone who would listen, "How does a woman dress when she's sporting man hands?" I can't wear my fluffy scarves; I'll have to do away with my cute and fashionable jackets; and so much for being bejeweled with an occasional *bling bling*.

With hands that look like dirty foam, I'll look like a drag queen in anything but bad denim and leather chaps. All I need to complete the look is a five o'clock shadow. Which—by the way—may not be too far off. Turns out the yellow foamy stuff also transfers and multiplies when one touches one's face.

There's a resolution in this somewhere, I just know it.

38

HOLD THAT DIET UNTIL
THE FUDGE IS GONE

I despise the TV programming this time of year. It's "weight-loss" this and "diet" that. Exercise more, eat less, and you'll work your derriere right down to a size six.

I wish.

I did some figuring the other day and calculated that I've lost a total of 1,148 pounds during my lifetime. By all accounts, I should be the size of Thumblina and proudly sporting a label that says, "fat free."

Now that I look back on the holidays, I realize that I should have limited the eggnog. While we're at it, it would have been a good idea to keep desserts to a minimum and any fool with half an ounce of restraint would have passed on the third helping of Mother's pea and egg salad. For Pete's sake! Who knew the peas would go straight to my thighs? My jeans feel tight, my belt screams to be let out a notch, and even my socks are starting to show signs of distress—and they're one-size-fits-all.

Generally speaking, I like to put off my post-holiday dieting until the fudge is gone. And I always think it's best to wait until after the Christmas cookies have been devoured to start counting calories. Then there's always the chocolate covered cherries from Aunt Mimsy to consider, the fruitcake that's gotta go, and hey! Those bourbon balls aren't going to eat themselves.

To make matters worse, my dear and delightful friend Karen made a glorious batch of Creamy Chocolate Eatmore Bars for the holidays this year.

(She used to be a gal I could count on.)

"Oh, they're so simple," she said with a smile on the day that she showed up at the door and motioned for her delivery boy to haul a carton of them in. "I just took a plethora of chocolate, a gallon of cream and folded it all together. It sounds quite fattening, but once you consider the calcium value, a 20 oz. serving provides all of the essential nutrients, protein and potassium that your body requires for the day. They're really quite healthy."

She didn't need to go on and on. Quite frankly, she had me at *plethora*.

She said they were for the family, but I hid them in the back of the freezer behind a bag of chicken gizzards and the kids didn't get so much as a whiff of them. It took me the better part of the holiday season to devour the lot of them by myself.

Now, desperate times call for desperate measures. So I called my good friend Louise yesterday and challenged her to a weight-loss contest.

"First one to lose 10 pounds," I said as I swallowed the last Chocolate Eatmore Bar, "buys the other one lunch."

"You're on," said Louise. "I'll come to your house on Wednesday at 9 a.m. We'll talk over strategies and then we'll weigh in."

She showed up promptly at 8:30 with a smile and a box of donuts. "What are those?" I asked as I eyeballed the double chocolate.

"One last hurrah before we commence to starving ourselves."

"I don't need a hurrah. I need will power. I'm starting to make a beeping sound when I back up."

"Oh, you are not. Besides, I know at least 10 women who are heavier than you are."

"Really?" I asked as I devoured half of a donut in one bite. "Name one."

"Well, my dear friend Zelda hasn't seen her toes since September."

"But Zelda is 8 months pregnant."

"Yeah, well, with a body like she had, we all knew she was bound to gain weight sometime."

I poured the coffee and added an abundance of cream. Then we toasted our new and healthy lifestyle with a cream-filled log and a silent prayer that Zelda would gain another five pounds in the labor room.

I started out with good intentions of losing weight. I watched Oprah's dietitian on TV, went to an exercise class, and even parked at the far end of Sunmart's parking lot.

Things were going splendidly—that is until my dear and darling friend Freda (whom I've always trusted) called to announce that she was bringing over a case of post-holiday Cookie Balls.

"I just crushed them and into a fine powder," she said as she set a case of them on the floor. "Then I added a pound of cream cheese and smothered them with chocolate—which just so happens to be a vegetable. I know it sounds fattening. But when you consider the nutritional value of the cream cheese, they're as healthy as a bowl of parsley snips."

Ah, shoot. Who really wants a size six derriere anyway?

39

TAKE THIS PILL AND RUN WITH THE PUPPIES

As I dragged my way across the kitchen floor the other morning, with high hopes of reaching the coffee pot, the kids moved around me in a frenzy.

My little Lawrence was unable to locate his homework. Huey was in a panic as he tried to find his shoes. Charlie had a note from the teacher that needed to be signed, and Vernon, my eldest and wisecracking child, loudly announced that not only were we running low on shampoo, but that the tube of toothpaste had been squeezed dry. How was he to polish his pearly whites under such extreme conditions?

A woman with more energy would have snapped to attention. She would have assessed the situation at hand and taken charge.

But I stood in the midst of it all, sporting my baggy jammies and fuzzy purple slippers. I took a sip of caffeine and stared at my offspring. I must have been quite a sight. My eyes were still sporting last night's makeup, my hair pointed toward the heavens, and it was painfully obvious that my saddlebags were starting to get the best of me.

I pulled Lawrence's homework out from under a stack of newspapers, told Huey he had a spare pair of shoes under the trampoline, and signed Charlie's paper. He said it was a permission slip for a field trip. For all I knew, I could have been signing a consent form to donate my body to science. (Like they'd want it.)

I kissed each of the kids on the head as they passed by, bid a heart-felt farewell, and shooed them out the door with something along the lines of, "Make good choices and remember, Mommy loves!"

It was only 7:45 am, but I was exhausted. I turned on the television set and was about to rest my saddlebags in the nearest recliner when suddenly one of those drug commercials came on. This one featured a beautiful woman who pulls it all off because she's been prescribed Dynamism.

As her children finished up their four-course breakfast—including hand-squeezed juice—she efficiently packed them a hearty lunch. She moved about her kitchen (which by the way was clean) like a roller-skating Richard Simmons on caffeine.

When next she appeared on the screen, she was riding her bike in the forest. With her husband by her side, and the children trailing close behind, she was muscular, fit, and the epitome of what all women over forty want to look like. She may have had a gray hair or two, but that's only so other women will think, "Hey, I have gray hair. If I take Dynamism, I'll look great too."

She was happy, organized, and apparently on the brink of breaking a genetic code. Her husband looked at her with adoration and her kids were beaming with joy. It's as if the whole world was smiling because this woman is taking her Dynamism once a day.

The commercial never really says what Dynamism is for—although they'll list a simple side effect or two including heart arrhythmias and liver dysfunction. But while they're talking about these minor side effects, they show the stylish woman running in a field of poppies with her children and a puppy.

Next thing I knew I was thinking, "Hey, I want to take Dynamism so I can run in a field of poppies with the children and a puppy, too. I wonder what size her waist is?" I didn't care about the side effects. They seemed insignificant when compared to the bliss this woman had in her life. And then, just for a bit of added reassurance, the announcer said something to the tune of, "Hey, the side effects are serious, but they're pretty much the same as placebo."

Then he lowered his voice, and spoke in a tone that was husky, hushed, and downright sentimental. He sounded as if he was close to tears as he asked, "Shouldn't you ask your doctor if Dynamism is right for you?"

"So, what do you think?" I asked my doctor. "Is Dynamism right for me?"

"Lori, Dynamism is for seasonal allergies."

"And?"

"And, you don't suffer from seasonal allergies."

"But the woman on TV had happy children, a perky hair-do, AND a clean kitchen."

"Lori..."

"If I had seasonal allergies, could you give me the pill then?"

"Tell you what, here's a prescription for a multivitamin."

"Will it give me the energy to run with puppies and travel through the forest with the children?"

"No, but the saleswoman from the drug company that presented it to me did have a great award winning smile."

"Great. I'll take it. Now, what do you have for saddlebags?"

40

ANOTHER DRIVER'S LICENSE PHOTO CASUALTY

I picked up the phone the other day to call the doctor's office so I could set up an appointment for my annual physical.

I might have even made the call if it hadn't been for one thing: I didn't want to.

There's nothing I hate more than the annual physical. It's neither the time it kills, nor the suffering and pain. It is knowing that I have to weigh on their dang scale. Without fail, it puts me in at 15 pounds more than any other scale I come in contact with throughout the year. It makes me feel fat just thinking about it.

After careful consideration, I decided to put it off until I shed my winter weight. I set the phone down and was about to walk away when my good friend Louise called in a state of despair.

She was absolutely frantic as she explained that she had just renewed her driver's license. "This photo is the most humbling picture anyone has taken of me in my entire life!" she cried into the phone. "It makes me look as if I'm a fugitive from justice."

"Oh, Louise, it can't be that bad."

"It is that bad. I can't believe that I'm going to have to flash this ID at people for the next five years. I'm telling you, there should be laws against deflating a gal's self esteem and then charging her $23 for it."

She had asked the gal at the DMV, "How can your camera possibly turn out this kind of picture? Do you pride yourselves on making decent people look hideous?"

"Well," the lady replied, "I think it turned out OK."

"Don't tell me you think this looks like me. My face is fat and blobbish, my complexion is ruddy, and I look as if I have twelve chins, for Pete's sake!"

"I could put a hologram on your face," the lady said smugly.

"Would that make it more slender?"

"No, but it might distract an observer."

"I don't want to distract observers. I want to look like me. This picture makes me look as if someone goosed me with a cattle prod the second you snapped the photo."

"Perhaps you had a frightening thought."

"Perhaps your camera is possessed," Louise replied. "All I know is I'm going to have to walk the straight and narrow for the next several years, because I'll be doggoned if I'll show this picture to a law enforcement officer or anyone else for that matter."

I tried my best not to laugh at dear Louise when she stopped by later to show me the new ID. "Well," I said as nicely as possible, "I've seen worse."

"Are you stinking kidding me?" she asked with dismay. "My nose looks as if it's out of alignment, my smile is off center, and what do you suppose happened to my hair? I swear it looked good when I went in there, but the gal on my ID looks like Phyllis Diller on a bad hair day. Tell me I don't look like this."

"Did you mean to make a grimace?"

"No, I think the camera intentionally failed to take full advantage of my photogenic qualities. For reasons we may never understand, that picture makes me look like a bloodhound intent on a kill. I look like Scarface. The Godfather. I look like Al-stinking-Capone. I could ward off a would-be attacker with this by saying, 'stand back or I'll show you my ID and—Buddy, trust me—you don't want that!'"

"It says here that you weigh 115 pounds."

"Well, yes. Nobody puts their real weight down. Why would they? Now that I think about it, the only way this could get any worse is if the DMV had made me get on the scale. That would be as horrifying as going to the doctor's office. In fact, I'm surprised they don't combine my driver's license renewal with an annual physical and then I could get all of my humiliation over in one fell swoop."

Suddenly I forgot all about Louise's bad picture and thought of my own predicament. "Louise, this is a legal document, right?"

"As legal as my last will and testament. Why?"

"Because I think I'm going to call my doctor's office and make my appointment for a physical after all. I'll simply bypass the scale as I tell them, 'I weigh 120, and I've got legal documentation right here that says so.'"

41

QUICK TRIP TURNS INTO
$257 SHOPPING SPREE

If I hadn't needed both groceries and toiletries at the same time, I would never have ended up in a super center in the first place. That's for stinking sure.

But we all know what happens when the milk runs dry and the kids are forced to use baking soda as a toothpaste substitute. It makes a parent unpopular, to say the least. I had entertained the notion of waiting for the supplies until our eldest child came home. I mean, isn't that why we let him turn 16 in the first place—so that he could fill in for the occasional "milk run?"

But the truth is that I've barely seen him since he became old enough to man a vehicle. I do enjoy an occasional glimpse of him as he runs through the house now and then, grabbing a fresh shirt and something that may or may not be clean socks. And once in a while a child, who appears to be a man, will surface in front of me and ask for the gas card. What the moment lacks in bonding, it makes up for in frustration.

That bounced the ball of responsibility back into my court. Once the family heard I was going to a super center, they jumped for joy, checked their supplies, and expanded my list. They needed ballpoint pens, body spray, basketball polish, AAA batteries, and any shampoo that didn't have feminine words on it—like balancing or fortifying.

I'm not certain, but I suspect that things went awry as soon as I pulled into the parking lot of the super center. Because, I still don't know how it is that a person can go in for a few simple supplies and a box of pens and come out an hour later having spent $257.

I had even set my jaw firmly. I'd adjusted my waistband and lectured myself in a stern voice, "Get in and get out. Pick up the shampoo while you're in the toothpaste section, sweep through the office supply aisle for the pens, and to get the economy-sized pack of toilet paper before the shopping side of the brain even knows we are in the store." It sounded good in theory.

Yet, despite my self-reassurance, I knew I would be unable to refrain. I walked through the doors slower than a kid going to clean the john.

Some say it's the color of the tile at the super centers. Others blame it on the smell. My good friend, Mabel, swears that when the greeter smiles and inquires, "How ya doin'?" it's actually a subconscious phrase for, "Now that you're here, you might as well stock up."

At the risk of sounding paranoid, I must say that I strongly suspect that they've piped subliminal messages into the music. Because while I thought I was listening to, "Bye-bye Baby, Bye-bye" on the loud-speaker, I'm fairly convinced that on some level I heard a low and rather husky voice inquire, "Say girl, how's your mayonnaise and your mustard? Aren't your hair supplies waning? You've always wanted one of those wet-jet mops and—oh look!—they're on sale!"

While I was in the shampoo section and listening to a bad remake of "Copacabana" that was coming through the overhead speakers, I'm quite certain the subliminal voice insisted, "If you loved your children, you'd buy them new coats, and what about your poor husband? He looks raggy to say the least. For a mere $18.98 you could not only update his wardrobe, but you could buy him the socks of his dreams."

By the time I'd returned home, I was loaded down on enough soaps and detergents to start a janitorial service. I'd purchased coats, clothing, undergarments, and a plethora of socks. I put away the office supplies, loaded the bread drawer, and couldn't wait to try out my new-fangled broom.

Just then a child—who may or may not have been our eldest—appeared before my eyes. "Hey Mom, did you remember to get deodorant?"

"No, but I did get this cute and stylish blouse."

"Oh, good luck with that," he replied as he turned up his nose. "Can I have the keys to the car?"

"Where are you going?"

"Back to the super center to get deodorant."

"Okay, but try not to look at the tile while you're in there. And for Pete's sake, don't smell anything. Here's a set of earplugs just to be safe. Oh, and whatever you do, do NOT say hello to the greeters."

42

NO REST FOR THE WEARY ON HOMEWORK

Some say the arrival of their children after school can be overwhelming. The euphoria, the excitement, the sheer volume, why, it's enough to make some mothers jump right out of their ankle socks. It's like standing in a tub of water and having someone drop in an electrical appliance. It can certainly give one a heck of a jolt.

Just yesterday—despite the fact that I was three feet in front of one of the little dears—he repeatedly shouted at the top of his lungs, "I'm home!"

"Did you miss us?" inquired another as he performed 13 vertical leaps in less than ten seconds. "Did you miss us, huh, huh, huh? How 'bout now?"

Yet, I'm actually more overwhelmed by the homework—the late nights, the last minute projects. In fact I'm still trying to recover from the bad grade I got on my son's English paper in 1999.

I've completed my formal education and obtained all of the wisdom I need to get through the average day. Although I'm no guru, I know most of my states and capitols, can readily explain the difference between a noun and a verb, and can calculate the exact amount of ointment that it takes to soften my corns.

Still, I have to be the tutor for history, the flash card queen of reading, and the mentor for photosynthesis. Why, I've even been known to do a math problem or two. Just so long as it wasn't above the third grade level and the metric system wasn't involved.

Recently, I was reviewing *Your Endocrine System and You* with the eldest, when my darling Lawrence appeared at my elbow.

"Mom," he said as he dropped a sixty-pound science book on my lap, "my solar system is due in a couple of days. I'm going to need you to brush up on your knowledge of the upper atmosphere—and how are you with Neptune?" (Like I'm going to pull that little feather of wisdom out of my hat.)

"I think Neptune clearly falls into your father's line of knowledge." I replied.

"Dad helped me study for my Congress test. He said it's your turn."

"Did you tell him I helped your brother understand the three distinct phases of fungi life cycles and have made vast preparations for President's Day?"

"No, but he won't care because he had to help Vernon do an in-depth study on primitive cultures."

"Dang it," I said as I gave in to defeat, "I forgot about what he did with the Neolithic Ages."

I tried my best to get out of it, and you can look down on me if you want to, but who really wants to spend a night analyzing solar systems and determining which planets have gas.

It's enough to make a gal choke on her coffee.

Not wanting to let my child down, and unable to pass the responsibility to his father, I helped Lawrence obtain information from a web site entitled, *The Earth as a Peppercorn*. Then I took him out to purchase the necessary items. We had just arrived at the store when my precious Little Charlie called and inquired, "Mom, when are you coming home?"

"Just as soon as we can find a ring for Saturn. Why?"

"Because I just remembered, I need one

hundred signatures for my 100-day party at school tomorrow."

"Charlie," I said as I experienced a tightening in my chest, "how long have you known about this?"

"Since last Thursday."

"Last Thursday? But today is Tuesday."

"I know, and tomorrow's Wednesday and that's why I need it today."

"Why didn't you tell me sooner?"

"Because you didn't ask."

"Charlie, how would I know to ask?"

"Because Mom's are supposed to ask."

Allow me to add that to the list of my shortcomings. As if I weren't still suffering inadequacies from the project we turned in on cell respiration.

After purchasing paints, wires, and a plethora of Styrofoam balls, I headed home to get the dang signature book so that I could travel abroad and ask for autographs like a desperate employee of the paparazzi.

I was about to head out the door when a child appeared at my side. "Mom," he inquired, "how are your decimals?"

Finally, someone was concerned about my well being. "Well honey," I replied as I touched his sweet little concerned face, "it's so nice that you asked. My feet are killing me and I could really go for a little 'R and R' right now."

"Whatever," he said as he rolled his eyes, "have a seat right here and I'll go and get my math book."

43

HOW WAS YOUR DAY? BETTER NOT ASK

Although I can't brag much about intellect, I can boast about my imagination. In fact, I can conjure up images on a whim. I like to imagine that I'm rich, thin, and that my house is clean. Just yesterday I imagined that my hair did what I wanted it to and to celebrate the moment, I took the afternoon off and went shopping.

Sometimes, however, imagination is all that I have. Take the other day, for instance, when my husband—the carpenter—came home from work and told me, "We've finished erecting the structural members of the building, back framed the truss system, and hopefully we'll be able to feed in the hip roof before day's end tomorrow."

While I'm very sure that what he just described involved a great amount of planning and perhaps even a bit of math, I could only imagine men with hard hats, hammers and a pile of Lincoln logs.

I simply smiled, nodded and pretended to understand. The poor man had spent days constructing a new building and for all I know he could have been ordering a bowl of fresh peaches in Latin.

I read somewhere, long ago, that a spouse should show interest in their mate's career. Smiling here and nodding there. Listening where necessary. Offering a sympathetic ear and—on occasion—extending some unsolicited advice.

But that was way back in my pre-children days. Perhaps as far back as a time when I still believed *Cosmopolitan* had all the answers to marriage with an article entitled, "How to Keep Your Man Interested."

Back then I thought I should learn all there was to know about his line of work. In fact, I'd planned on learning all about it right up until the moment that he told me he was installing a cantilever overhang.

Well, color me stupid! Up until that moment, I could have sworn a cantilever was a fancy name for a decorative lighting fixture that is suspended from a ceiling.

I can't help but wonder if other people have trouble understanding what it is, exactly, that their spouses are talking about. I wonder if Eve prefaced dinner with, "How was your day, Dear?" And I wonder if Adam answered in a language that she couldn't understand, explaining in detail the horror and errors of the day he just put in.

Eve must have felt frustrated as she whipped up a stellar fruit salad and listened to Adam babbling on. "Well, I named all of the mammals, and then got started on the invertebrates. Tomorrow I plan on classifying the amphibians and the primates, but I'll be darned if I know what labels I'm going to come up with for the canines. How was your day?"

"Well, I'm not sure if my fig leaves will hold out until the spring, and the garden is a mess. Here Adam, have an apple."

I can only imagine the intriguing conversation as medical people share their day with their spouses, "Sorry I'm late dear. My last patient suffered from Supraventricular Tachycardia requiring immediate Synchronized Cardioversion to prevent further myocardial ischemia. What a day!"

Worse yet, imagine being married to a police officer, "I had to run code on a 10-34 in progress, a 10-90J2 threatening 10-65, and wouldn't you know it...just before we're 10-97 they advise 10-22! Can you even stinking believe that?"

That's a big 10-4 on that one good buddy.

I suppose that we are all behooved to ask the spouse about their day and pretend that we understand the response.

"Well, the plumb Bob got stuck in the sump pump," my husband explained the other day, "and it was a booger to get it back out. The cement wouldn't set, the pathogenic device broke down, and I'll be danged if the pneumatic tools didn't pick that precise moment to call it a day. You have no idea what I'm saying, do you?"

"Yes, 'Bob' has been interfering with your pumping, your power screed had a bad day, and you'll be dog-goned if your air guns didn't pick that exact minute to act up."

"Say, that's not too bad. How was your day?"

"Well," I said trying to sound as distinguished and scholarly as possible, "our descendants have been captivated with an intriguing pursuit of arm-to-arm combat, and we're running low on calcium supplementation."

"Calcium supplementation? Wouldn't that be milk?"

"If you insist on being so obtuse as to call it that."

He's got nothing on me. He may have a complicated job, but I've got an imagination.

44

SOMETIMES A BAD MEMORY COMES IN HANDY

My dear and precious mother stopped by not long ago for coffee and a nice visit. While I added an abundance of cream to the brew, I said, "You know, Mom, Pat and I would love to get away for a couple of days. How's about you and Dad taking the boys for us some weekend?"

When she didn't respond, I turned to see that she had grabbed a *Country Living* magazine and had buried her face in it. It was nothing new—she's used this tactic on me many times before. (Especially when it comes to taking care of the kids.)

"Oh my gosh!" She exclaimed as she looked at the pages. "Have you seen this? Look at what this woman has done with her mudroom. Why, it's all dried flowers and basil and who would ever have thought to do that with a pair of galoshes?"

"Just think," I replied, as I ignored the fact she was ignoring me, "Dad, the kids, you, and a weekend of ESPN—why it's every grandparent's dream. Dad could take the boys to the park for the afternoons and buy them ice cream. Give the man a pipe and he could play Fred MacMurray while you spend your evenings enjoying scavenger hunts and the sound of a bouncing basketball."

"Fred MacMurray had three sons not four, and would you look at this red Fiesta Ware pitcher? I can't believe you haven't shown me this magazine before."

"For Pete's sake!" I said with frustration, "You've already seen that magazine! Now give it to me."

"I've never seen this magazine before in my life," she said as she clutched it to her chest.

"The heck you haven't. It's your magazine. You gave it to me in the first place!"

"You're making that up."

"Mother," I said as I grabbed it from her and turned it over, "your name is on the mailing label."

"Now do you see why I can't keep the children?" she said, finally addressing the issue. "I'm old, I have no memory."

"You can't blame that on age. In fact, I'm quite certain it's genetic and you've passed it on to me. I haven't been able to remember the children's names for years."

Memory is a funny thing, but I forget why.

I remember the days when I had one—but just barely. I can't exactly recall when my memory was still vital, but it seems like 1986 was a stellar year.

I distinctly remember an incident just last week—although it could have been in June—the phone rang and a woman asked, "Did you forget me?"

"That depends," I replied. "Who are you?"

"Lori!" she said with frustration, "It's Alice. I've been waiting for you to get back to me all afternoon."

"Oh yeah. Right. Alice. I'm so sorry. It's just been crazy. Alice who?"

She should know better than to place that kind of pressure on a woman who hides eggs for her own Easter egg hunt.

The worst thing about a bad memory is I can recognize faces, but can't remember names to save my soul. "Lori," (I'm often asked by some well-meaning acquaintance,) "how are you? How are your boys? How's your house? Your car? Are your parents faring well?"

"Good," I reply. "We're all great. And how are you and all of your……things?" (Which is safe, because everyone has things. God forbid I should inquire about a puppy to a person who hates dogs.)

I also suffer from Phonesia —the affliction of dialing a phone number and forgetting who I was calling just as they answer. "Who's this?" I asked a cranky man just last week.

"What do you mean, 'who's this?' You called me!"

"Oh! Well then, perhaps you can tell me what it is that I want."

"What are you bothering me for?"

"I'm not sure."

I was thinking about pretending that I had the wrong number and simply hanging up when he said, "Hang on a minute and I'll get your mother."

I heard him set the phone down and shout out, "Your daughter is on the phone!"

Suddenly it all came back to me. "Mom," I said when she answered, "I was wondering if you could keep the kids on the weekend of the 12th?"

"Who is this?" she replied.

"It's Lori."

"Art, do we have a daughter named Lori?"

"That depends," Dad answered, "what does she want?"

"She wants us to keep her kids on the weekend of the 12th."

"Hang up on her. It's probably one of those money-making schemes."

"I'm sorry Dear, we don't remember who you are. You'll have to take your kids elsewhere—perhaps to someone younger." And with that she promptly hung up.

Turns out a bad memory can be a good thing.— that is, if you're my mother.

45

TIME TO PURGE
THE HOLIDAY LEFTOVERS

Cleaning comes in at 93 on a scale of 1-100 of my favorite things to do—right in between flogging mice and hanging sheet rock.

Therefore, I like to start off my spring cleaning much the same way each year—by putting it off until the fall.

In moments of desperation, I have been known to dab a little Pine-Sol behind my ears, fill the washer with bleach, and put the vacuum in the middle of the living room so it'll appear as if I was about to use it.

What I lack in productivity I can certainly make up for with creativity.

Usually I save the dirty deed of deep cleaning for the occasional out-of-town visitor, or the loss of an item of such extreme importance that life itself would halt unless there is a quick recovery. Take last summer, for instance, when the boys lost their pet turtle in their bedroom. The search and seizure sparked a cleaning frenzy that lasted well into October.

Things are going to be different this year, however. I've been inspired to give spring cleaning a stellar go because of a woman I saw on a TV program called *The Grime Busters*. An entire team showed up on her doorstep and began to de-clutter and organize. They brought with them carpenters, spray painters, and a woman who could create a focal point in the living room out of a few twigs and a pack of chewing gum.

They not only fought against the intrusion of mess and muck, but single handedly rid her kitchen of litter and beat her bookcase-blahs. The transformation was to die for.

I decided that if I'm ever to bask in the glow of a clean and organized existence, I was going to have to rise to the occasion and purge like a pro. My sinks lacked luster, the garbage disposal was coughing, and it was high time someone stepped up to the plate and tossed out the Christmas leftovers.

I took the time to reassure myself that there is a God and that he wouldn't leave me in my hour of need. I hummed three stanzas of "We Shall Overcome" and headed to the kitchen.

It was there I found myself asking some very important questions such as: Am I the only human alive who didn't know that behind the back of the fridge one can grow a mass of dirt three inches thick? Am I the only one who didn't know this is the exact area where pennies replenish themselves, milk caps reproduce, and paper clips vacation for the winter? And what kind of sticky compound joined in and bonded the entire community in perfect harmony?

I'm fairly certain a lesser woman would have assessed the situation and promptly balked at the condition of the filth—as she shoved that bad boy back into its spot and pretended she never saw it.

But not me. No sir. I did exactly as my mother taught me to do. I waited until one of the children got out of hand and then I doled that chore out as punishment.

"Who cleans behind a refrigerator?" screamed my 12-year-old son, as if he were in a great deal of pain.

"Children who misbehave."

"But I'll go back and wash my toothpaste down

the sink—I promise."

"Too late for that now, Little Mister. Bad choices have bad consequences."

"Where did all of these alphabet magnets come from?"

"They were a present from your Grandmother when your oldest brother went to pre-school."

"But that was like 100 years ago."

"Turns out cleaning back here hasn't been on our annual 'to do' list."

"But you can't leave me with this mess. I'm only a child and there are laws."

"Yes, but the laws don't apply here. If you don't believe me, ask your older brother. He failed miserably on a case he tried against me last summer when the garbage can was ripe."

"But the Bible says to remember the Sabbath and keep it holy."

"That might hold water if it were Sunday. Here are your rubber gloves, your scrub brush, and a can of industrial-strength cleaner."

"I don't know anything about industrial-strength cleaners."

"Great, then it will be a learning experience as well as a productive one."

With that settled, I turned on my heel and headed back to my easy chair. "Filthy Makeovers" was coming on and I couldn't wait to see what they had in store for a farmhouse in Montana.

46

OH, NO! HERE COMES THE PRINCIPAL!

I'd like to state for the record that our school principal is a great man—a real happy-go-lucky sort of guy—always there with a "hello," anxious to assist with the door, and quick to snap and point whenever I get out of line.

I just don't like to see the man heading in my general direction.

Whenever I pick up the children and notice he is coming my way, I know it's going to be bad news. He never strolls by the vehicle just to see how I'm doing. He never raps on the window of the car to shoot the breeze, and he has never—not even once—stomped up and down in the middle of the street for no reason.

So when I see him approaching, I can rest assured something has become rotten in Denmark.

I hate getting into trouble with the principal. It completely ruins all the efforts I've put forth to establish a reputation as a model citizen. I can take the kids to church, practice good discipline, and follow Dr. Hasnokids' *Seven Steps of Bringing up God's Creatures*. Yet all of my hard work goes out the window the instant one of my precious dears pulls a prank.

Although our children aren't common criminals, they have been known to cause a minor disturbance now and then. They have disrupted snack time, picked on classmates, and—heaven forbid—have been caught chewing on a wad of gum big enough to choke a horse. I try not to let it get me down. In fact, I'm quite certain it only happens because they take after their adoring father.

When I saw the principal walking my way the other day, I quickly picked up a state map and buried my face in it. I was just coming off a long afternoon of paperwork and errands and I didn't want to hear anything he had to say.

As he knocked at the window, I abruptly cranked up the music on the radio and simply pretended he wasn't there.

Yet, he was persistent in his knocking. "Lori," he said firmly, "I know you can hear me, now roll down the window."

Feeling I had no choice, I slowly rolled the window down about two inches.

"I'd love to chew the fat with ya, but turns out something screwy has happened with the solar system and according to my horoscope, I'm to avoid all authority figures today."

"That's very interesting," he said in a tone that indicated he thought otherwise. "Did you receive my phone call this afternoon?"

"Would I be here if I had?"

"I need to talk to you about your son."

"Are you sure it was my son? You know, if you put enough mud and dirt on those boys, they all tend to look alike."

"I'm quite certain it was your boy I summoned to the office today," he said looking quite serious.

I gave him my God-knows-I-did-the-best-I-could look and said through the crack, "Will we need legal representation?"

"No," he replied. "We have a new boy who is looking at our institution and we'd like one of your boys to accompany him for a day."

I couldn't believe it. I darn near choked on my breath mint and said, "Well, why didn't you say so in the first place? Of course our precious child would be happy to show this young man our school. He could take him around, introduce him to his friends, and—if you'd like—we could even have him show this lad a few of his tricks."

"Let's not get carried away. I'd just like your son to make him feel welcome."

A week or so later the principal showed up at our front door. By that time, I'd forgotten all about the touring day. So when I viewed his stern look through the peep-hole, my stomach jumped into my throat. The usual anxiety filled my chest, my breathing stopped, and I could barely muster a swallow.

"We're not in right now," I said after I'd opened the door a crack, "but if you'll leave a message, we'd be happy to get back to you."

"Are you done?"

"That depends. But I don't think my boys did it this time. We've been having them eat all of their vegetables, they've been getting good rest, and saying prayers daily for world wide peace, amen."

"Good, I just wanted to tell you your son did a fine job for our school yesterday. He showed great social skills, was kind and considerate, and really came through. We're honored to have him as a student."

I'm not fully convinced it was my kid he was talking about. But I tell you this, if the child he spoke of was mine, then one thing's for sure:

He totally takes after me.

47

YOUNG CELL PHONE FAN STUCK AT POINT D

Our eldest son Vernon has relentlessly been pleading his case for a cell phone for over a month now.

He's placed sticky notes throughout the abode, left advertisements on the steering wheel, and—just last week—he posted a large sign in the living room that said, "Add a line for $9.95."

"Analyze with me," he said to his father and me the other night as he pointed to his homemade chart with a laser pen. "The two of you could be at point A, lingering in despair. Meanwhile, I may be as far away as point C or even D. Now imagine for me, if you will, that you suddenly had in indescribable desire to contact me. How would you go about it?"

I raised my hand, and when he called my name I asked, "Are we calling you to bring home a gallon of milk?"

"You could be."

"Perhaps," I continued with excitement, "we're calling you to see if you can swing by and pick Charlie up from the ballpark."

(I just love it when he picks Charlie up from the ballpark.)

"Mother," he said as he rolled his eyes, "you're missing the point. Without a cell phone I can do none of these things."

"I could give you a list before you go," I replied enthusiastically.

"What if I lose the list?"

"I could send you subliminal messages."

"Mom, you're sucking the wind right out of my demonstration. I think it's time the two of you ask yourselves, 'What's it gonna take to put our child into a cell phone today?'"

I suppose I can understand his frustration. After all—according to him—our son is the one and only kid in the entire school who doesn't have his own form of high-tech communication in his back pocket. Why, without polyphonic ringtones and instant text messaging, he can barely show his face in English class.

Have we no shame?

"I could be stranded at point D indefinitely," he said in conclusion as he clutched his chest. "I'd have no hope of ever being able to contact the outside world again. The thought we should all ponder is this: Is there no concern for my safety?"

"He gets this from you," my husband said after Vernon left the room.

"Me? What did I do?"

"You campaigned for a cell phone like a lobbyist on Capitol Hill."

"But I need my cell phone."

"Name a situation where you need your cell phone."

"Well, take last week, for instance, when you couldn't find the remote. Or how about last Tuesday when Huey had an inquiry with regards to his biology exam, or that day when Charlie needed 28 soup labels in order to pass the first grade."

"We would have survived."

"You people wouldn't have been able to make it across the floor."

Later, I was enjoying time alone and scrubbing a pan when Vernon appeared at my elbow. He had obviously given up on pleading and had decided to pull out all stops with another strategy: The Eddie Haskell Approach.

"I'm going to need you on my side with this one, Mom," he said as he gave me a hug. "You have an award-winning style and the perfect touch with Dad. I'll tell ya what I'm gonna do. I'm going to be your right-hand man. I'll help you with the dishes, dust the ceiling fans, and I'll even do a sink scrubbing at no extra charge. What do ya say?"

"Will you throw in a mop job as well?"

"I'll make it look like Mr. Clean used this place for a demonstration."

"What talk do you want me to give him?"

"What do you got?"

"I've got the, *Things Will Always Look Better in the Morning*, my *What Comes Around Goes Around*, and then, of course, there's always the *Always Put on Clean Underwear lecture number 412c*—although I don't think that one is appropriate in this instance."

"How about if you simply give him your, *What's Good Enough for the Millers is Good Enough for Us* talk. That one packs a good wallop."

Later, as my husband watched his favorite TV shows, I hit him with it.

"Honey, what do you think about giving Vernon his very own cell phone?"

"I think it's expensive."

"Well, it is only $9.95 a month."

"Yeah, but if you take that times 12, it's $120 a year. We'd be out 1,200 bucks by the end of the decade and on the brink of bankruptcy by the time we reach retirement. Of course, if you were willing to make the sacrifice and give him your cell phone...."

"Now that you mention it," I interrupted him, "I think you may be right. We might be money ahead to just leave that kid at point D."

48

BUT HONEY, IT'S
A SMALL DUMP TRUCK

When my beloved husband first mentioned the prospect of building a new home in the country, I have to admit I was intrigued. A little place far away from it all. Gentle breezes, tranquil nights, and the blissful sounds of tumbleweeds as they lodged themselves in the chicken wire fences.

Then he enlisted my help with the building process, and that, my dear friends, is when things changed. He used to be a perfectly good companion. He was the kind of guy who would open the doors for me and give me his coat when I was chilled. He'd fix me a sandwich, pour my coffee, and—if the timing were right—he'd touch my knee as he asked me to pass the salt.

Time changed all of that. By challenging my anything-a-man-can-do-I-can-do side, my husband has turned me into a lipstick toting construction worker. Over the course of the past year, I've endured horrendous days in extreme conditions, doing things no woman would want to do. I've poured concrete, installed windows, and worn cover-alls that made me look like a she-man.

All I needed to complete the look was a tattoo of an anchor on my forearm.

I feel I've been a pretty good sport about it all. Oh, sure, I've done my share of cursing in the sub-zero temperatures. But you'd complain, too, if you were hanging insulation in a Gortex suit.

At first I put my foot down when it came to the operation of the heavy equipment. "But it's a small dump truck," he said of the oversized vehicle that sat on the driveway.

"I won't drive it," I replied, "and you can't make me."

I'm not sure how he did it—perhaps it was his charm. It could be his award-winning style. Most likely he said something that once again appealed to my stubborn streak. All I know is within the hour I found myself smack dab in the middle of a sandpit, trembling as I got my back box filled to the brim by an enormous loader. I sat in the cab with my eyes shut, shaking like a leaf as I clutched my purse and rued the day.

"That's it!" I said sternly when he came home for dinner. "I won't be cajoled into driving that thing. I'll swing a hammer, bend the rebar, but I won't drive that oversized beast."

"No more dump trucks?" he asked as if I'd just hurt his feelings.

"No more dump trucks." I replied roughly.

He's left me alone about it until just recently. "I wonder where I could find a strong willed person," he said as he watched me out of the corner of his eye, "to drive the dump truck to the bottom of that hill to get a load of fill dirt."

"Drive that beast to the bottom of the hill?" I exclaimed with disbelief. "You're messing with me, right?" Driving the truck on city streets was one thing. But taking it down an overwrought cow trail meant for tractors and farm implements—that's quite another.

Before I knew it I was once again climbing into the cab. I tossed in my purse, checked my hair and applied a fresh coat of lipstick. I may have been driving a dump truck, but there was no sense in looking like an animal.

As I was bringing the rig back up the hill, a feeling of power overcame me. I had the truck in first gear and it was giving me all it had. When the time was right, I put it into 2nd gear and as I rounded the corner, I leaned to the right in hopes that the truck wouldn't roll over to the left. When I reached the summit, I backed that bad boy up into a two-point turn and pressed on full steam ahead.

My beloved spouse turned and looked at me as I drove it home. I was sure our eyes locked and the bond between us strengthened. I just knew the look he was giving me was one of love and adoration. When I saw him say something to our son, Lawrence, I'd imagined it was something along the lines of, "Did I marry a great gal or what?"

I was beaming with pride. I'd taken on the odds and I'd won. What more could I have asked of myself?

I hopped down out of the cab and Lawrence ran to my side. "Your Dad is quite the romantic, isn't he Honey? What did he say when he saw how I was handling that truck?"

"Well," said Lawrence, "Dad said, 'your mother's getting braver, but she didn't get a full load of dirt.'"

I think I'm going to have to bite the bullet and get that tattoo.

49

MOM'S CRABBY 'TIL SOMEONE BUYS THE HOUSE

You know the trouble with some women? They are too clean. I once had a friend with a neat house and I didn't like her. Hanging out with her was like experiencing a fat day and chumming with Pamela Lee.

It's hard to befriend a woman whose beds are always made, whose windows are always clean, and who brings along a plethora of antibacterial wipes whenever she comes to visit.

Personally, I've always let my home get grubby out of love for my children. I'm a much better person when I'm not stressing that someone will smear jelly on my white, sterile walls or—heaven forbid—unalphabetize the soup cans.

Things have always gone just splendidly with our not-so-neat-lifestyle. Right up until the minute we decided it was time to put our home on the market.

It was a moment to regenerate, reinvigorate, and—if time would allow—regurgitate at the prospect of living in an endless state of purification.

I worked day and night on organizing the closets. I rid the bedrooms of debris and I cleaned the windows to a shimmering shine. I ran around with a broom in my hand and a dust rag in my pocket for two weeks straight. Sweeping here, knocking down cobwebs there, and on occasion, chasing a chocolate-toting boy back into the kitchen.

I wiped down the walls, polished the cabinetry, and actually took on the aggressive leftovers in a lengthy battle and won.

At the end of my cleaning session, the house glistened, it shone, it simply screamed, "BUY ME!"

Satisfied that the place looked as though it had never been lived in, I called my good friends over to view it.

"What are you trying to do?" my friend Karen asked as she walked through the kitchen, "ruin things for the rest of us?"

"Yes," exclaimed Louise, "if my husband lays eyes on this place, I'm ruined!"

Mable was less subtle and went straight to the heart of things. "All right, Girl," she said with a penetrating glare, "spit it out. Where did you stash the dirty socks?"

Although I'd forewarned them, I was foolish to think the children would be transformed as they resided in our sterile home. In fact, I was stupid enough to believe they'd stop dead in their tracks on occasion and pay homage to the sparkling foyer.

Instead they left their backpacks in the living room, thumbed their noses at the fake zinnias, and shed their clothing all the way down the hall. I even caught my precious Little Charlie waltzing around the corner with an over-sized bag of Marshmallow Mateys.

Who eats Marshmallow Mateys in a dust-free room that has been adorned with greenery? Have they no shame?

Although I feel it's justified, I suppose this new and clean style of living has left me somewhat testy. It's hard giving home tours to complete strangers at a moment's notice.

Perhaps it was a bit much when I installed a crumb alarm system in the kitchen and penalized the children for undergarments that were strewn about the front lawn. But no mother worth her salt can keep a home this clean amidst the chaos without getting just a little bit crotchety.

Yesterday my husband crept past the kitchen as though he were behind enemy lines.

"What's the matter with you?" I asked.

"I was afraid I'd upset you."

"Upset me? Why on earth would you be afraid of that?"

"Well, I think I can speak for us all when I say you have been a little obsessed with this cleaning business lately."

"Obsessed?" I asked as I plucked a microscopic piece of lint off of his shirt. "Why would you say such a thing?"

"Well, you've taken to hiding things every time someone comes up the walk. I've discovered shoes in the towel drawer, dirty dishes in the oven, and last night while you were sleeping you screamed out, 'shove the socks in the truck!' As if that weren't bad enough, yesterday you swept a pile of cookies under the rug."

"So, what's wrong with that?"

"I was eating them at the time."

Once this place sells and we're in our new home, I'll have to take a break from cleaning and go back to my old ways. A gal has to let the house get grubby now and then. Not for herself you understand, but for the sake of her family.

50

LAWNMOWERS SHOULD NEVER GO THUNK

If I had it all to do over again, I would never have become a lawn-mowing individual. I would have remained indoors, enjoyed a temperature-controlled environment, and waited for the finish coat on my nails to set as I watched my husband mow the yard.

But I ruined it all for myself early on in our marriage. I was getting by without mowing right up until the moment that I noticed my beloved had missed a spot. Looking back I know I should have kept my mouth shut and let the yard turn into a wildlife habitat.

I guess I didn't realize that a cute comment combined with a critical eye would land me a life-long lawn job and custody of the family compost container.

It's not that I'm obsessive about lawn mowing, but I do prefer a yard with even borders. I adore green acres, trimmed hedges, and the luxury of a few hardy perennials as they germinate in the formulated soil. And if I were ever to be awarded Yard of the Week, it would complete my lists of top 20 things to accomplish before I die.

Therefore, it was no small sacrifice when I let one of my little cherubs mow the lawn the other day. I would just as soon have been outside basking in the horticulture as opposed to staring out the window and hoping he'd mow it right.

But it has been my goal for many a year to raise sons my future daughters-in-law would thank me for. Men who could whip up an omelet, put away shaving cream, and mow the back 40 as their load of whites spin out in the rinse cycle. Therefore, I bit my lip and told my little dear to do the best he could.

In case you're not familiar with a little boy's style of mowing, I'll describe it for you with a few colorful adjectives: spasmodic, irregular, and downright lopsided.

Things did not go well. But it wasn't until I heard the proverbial THUNK that I realized how bad things had gone. I'm no mechanic, but I instantly knew that THUNK is not a good sound for a lawn mower to make. In fact, it's a bad sound that ranks right up there with hearing a stylist say, "oh-oh" as she trims the back of your hair.

I looked out into the yard to see the uneven grassland and a lawnmower which was smoking like a chimney.

I simply couldn't allow the yard to remain in a state of disorganization, so I loaded up a couple of the children and headed off to rent a mower.

Of course I couldn't get the replacement mower to start, so I stood out in the yard and tactfully summoned my eldest son by screaming his name repeatedly with frustration. "Veron! Vernon! Verrrrrnon!"

What I lacked in class I made up for with a lot of brass. Naturally Vernon was able to get it started with 20 to 25 quick pulls and left me happily mowing—right up until it was time to stop the engine and dump the grass.

Then, of course, the filthy beast wouldn't restart. I again summoned Vernon by standing in the yard, fist clenched, and hollering his name at the top of my lungs.

I'd calmed down by the time I'd watched him give the mower another 30 to 35 pulls. I was so relieved to hear the engine sputter that I patted

Vernon on the back, gave him a kiss on the cheek, and offered a quick, "Mommy loves."

With total determination and a plethora of stupidity, I decided to skip the manicured look and go for "good enough" by simply mowing the long spots. But....before I got even half done with achieving "good enough," that low life grass muncher died for good. I couldn't re-start it. Vernon couldn't re-start it and the poor-yet-strong passerby with a tattoo of an anchor on his forearm couldn't re-start it (even though he'd given it a good effort and called the klunker a few choice names.)

The lawnmower rental place was more than happy to replace the mower. Although they guaranteed the next lawnmower to start on the first yank, I was a bit discouraged by its appearance. The carriage was approximately 8 inches wide and the engine looked like it should blow bubbles out of its little top as it played show tunes and sang its way across the yard.

The new mower started all right. But do you think that piece of work would run for more than 30 seconds at any time?

Heck no!

Following a few more painful attempts to mow with a mower that wasn't mowing and a full blown temper tantrum that will forever leave me known around the neighborhood as "that crazy lady who stands in the yard and screams out 'Vernon' all day," I've decided yard work may not be for me after all.

Who really needs Yard of the Week anyway?

51

MOVING TO THE COUNTRY

I've recently found out that one receives a lot of flack from family and friends when one decides to move out of the city limits.

My sister, for example, thinks we're destined to be overcome by snakes. Some of our in-laws are certain we'll need a navigational system if we're ever to find our way out of the cornfields, and my mother is convinced that we'll be raising rabbits in no time.

But no one has been more troubled by our move than my good friend Karen. "Why would you even contemplate moving to the country?" she asked over enchiladas the other day. "Have you thought about what you are going to do when you run out of milk?"

"Well, you know there's a dairy just up the street."

"When you live in the country," she said matter-of-factly, "you don't get to have streets anymore. They're all roads. I tell ya, you're a city slicker at heart and yet you'll be mowin' with goats and sloppin' the pigs before year's end. And what about all of those last-minute treats for school, shortages on Cheese nips, and have you made any plans for when the well runs dry?"

The way Karen tells it, I'll soon be spending my days in the barnyard, wearing a sundress, and seed feeding chickens from my oversized apron as I sing Old MacDonald at the top of my lungs in an attempt to get the hens to lay.

"We'll plan ahead for the treats and Cheese nips," I said with more confidence than I felt. "And barter with the neighbors for water if the well runs dry. Besides, you'll be coming out to visit and you can bring out the supplies."

"We'll try to come out and visit when we can, but you know it's just so far out. I would have to get the oil changed in the van, check the tires, get out my atlas, and analyze the weather. Then I'd have to stock up on emergency supplies, get new windshield wipers, increase my car insurance, notify family members of my trip, take extra vacation days, get someone to water my flowers, bring in the mail, check the house, contact my neighborhood watch group to keep an eye on the place, get travelers checks, passports, get my shots updated, extend my cell phone minutes, stop the papers, stop the mail, get all my bills caught up, clean out the fridge so the milk won't spoil, lug out the luggage, pack, and get the laundry caught up. You know, I think it would just be easier to call you and see how you are doing."

"But, Karen," I replied, "we'll only be a few minutes from town."

"Yeah, well, a few minutes will turn into three days when it is blizzarding! Not to mention the black ice, snow, rain, and washed out roads. Why, you could be stranded out there for months and playing Swiss Family Robinson no less. I hope your husband has a good ax. It'll take upwards of 68 cords of wood to get you through the winter out there in God's country."

She left me contemplating many things—not the least of which was, *what the heck is a cord of wood?*

"Just you wait until the phone starts ringing," she wrote to me later in an e-mail. "How in the world will you tend to your children when they're in school in town and you're out in the middle of no where? I can just hear it now, 'Mom, I forgot my book. Mom, I forgot my paper. Mom, I need the permission slip or I can't go on the field trip. Mom, I forgot my lunch. Mom, you need to drive into town right away. You were supposed to bring three dozen carrots for Thanksgiving dinner at school.' And let's not forget the proverbial, 'Mrs. Clinch, you need to come to the principal's office. Your son (choose one) is in detention.' or 'Mrs. Clinch, your son has injured his toe. You must come quickly.' And you know it's only a matter of time before you answer the phone and hear an angry voice say, 'Mrs. Clinch, your son just snapped Mary's bra. We're going to have to ask you to report to the office at once.'"

    I suppose there's an air of truth to what she's saying. Yet there's still something that just draws me to live beyond the sidewalks.

    Meanwhile, I'd better use that navigational system to find me a cord of wood while there's still time.

52

NO TIME TO WORRY
ABOUT SKIN TONE

My skin care consultant called me the other day and said it was time to re-think my skin.

"With summer quickly approaching, we're going to have to work fast if we plan to revive your appearance. Your wrinkle patches need rejuvenated, your cuticles are dry, and if you don't start an exfoliation process soon, I swear, I won't even consider letting you link my name to your beauty regimen."

A couple of crinkles and a saggy chin and you'd think I was falling apart at the seams.

I told her I thought my regimen was doing fine. My skin stretches here, tugs there, and I'm fairly certain there was a time in February when I pulled on my cheek and it bounced back into place in less than a week.

"But you've got to be running low on the 37 step program we set you up with last fall," she said with disbelief. "It was only a 30-day supply."

I didn't know what to say. I still have an ample supply of Age-Fighting eye cream. My Facial Firming cream was still plentiful, and my jar of Nighttime Exuberance for the Middle Aged Vixen still sat unopened on the bathroom counter.

It's not my fault that I don't have time to worry about skin tone. How can a mother, such as myself, serve a husband, kids, an automatic dishwasher, and still have time to worry about exfoliation? I'm lucky to get the sheets pulled back before I fall into bed at night.

I suspect I have only myself to blame. I had good intentions of raising a family who could make their own toast. I'd planned on teaching them how to replace the toilet paper on the spool, pack their own lunches, and—when the time was right—I'd fully planned to conduct a sock-mating seminar.

Other women seem to manage so much better than I. My friend Estelle, for example, has time for both a beauty regimen and a freshly decorated home. Her children do their own homework, mate their own socks, and if her mornings unfold as she tells it, they load up into the car with smiles and head off for school like the Brady Bunch on Prozac.

I could really hate a woman like Estelle. Yet I couldn't help but be mesmerized.

"How the heck do you do it?" I asked as I resisted the urge to slap her.

"Well," she said as her ego shone through, "I start with the children and a white load every morning, and things just flow naturally from there. Hubert is in charge of changing the linens on Tuesday and Thursday. Mimsy cleans the windows after school, and if the floor is not vacuumed by 6 o'clock every evening, well, we've only young Hector to blame."

"What do you do if the children disobey?"

"Oh, they'd never disobey," she said as she went pale with the thought, "I forbid it."

She forbids it. Gosh, I wish I'd thought of that.

"Family," I said the very next night over supper, "things are going to change around here. My freedom is limited and my minutes are scarce. It's high time I free up some time and you are just the people to help me. Now what, if anything, can we as a family unit do to help out yours truly?"

My family reacted the same way they usually do with regard to meetings and change and that is with absolute horror.

"I have a list of names," I continued on as if my audience was attentive. "I also have an index of chores and a cute little roster of responsibilities for all of those involved. We'll start with the unloading of the dishwasher. Do I have any volunteers?"

"Vernon dirties more glasses than anyone," reported Huey. "I think he should be in charge of the dishwasher."

"Shut up, you little idiot," retorted Vernon. "You're the one who spends all of your time in the kitchen. You can do the dishwasher chore."

"Okay," I said, "It's time to move on to the bathroom list and the good news is that I have a fun little demo all lined up for this chore. Is anyone familiar with this?"

I was met with wide eyes and blank stares.

"This nifty little gadget," I said as I held up the toilet paper spool, "not only holds a roll of tissue but can be spun quite readily in the toilet paper distribution process. Would anyone like a presentation, or do you all think you are properly prepared to test out now?"

"I'd be confident to test out now," said Vernon. "Yet I'd prefer to test in an area that doesn't involve your bathroom. Your supplies are getting out of hand."

"Yeah," said Huey, "If you actually used some of that stuff you'd be as pretty as Estelle."

That's the funny thing about kids. They really bring things around to a full circle.

53

SO LONG TRANQUILITY, HELLO SUMMER

If I'm to believe the scuttlebutt about the abode, the school year is coming to an end. I'd like to sit and scowl. But what's a mother to do when the kids have been marking off days on the calendar, celebrating with laughter, and—on more than one occasion—have broken into a ceremonial dance?

It's a headache in progress.

Goodbye quiet mornings, early nights, and the tick-tock of the kitchen clock. Good riddance to flushed toilets, clean spaces, and the prospect of going for twenty minutes without hearing, "He's looking at me!"

So long tranquility, hello summer!

The past nine months went by in a whirlwind of extracurricular activities, scholastic affairs, and enough homework to have me choking on adverbs. I'd like to believe that it's a small price to pay to have the kids absent for several hours a day, but (and I know I'll kick myself for saying this) I simply can't wait for them to get out of school.

Some may color me crazy. Others will think me totally off my nut. They may even recommend a good strong pill and put me in a straight jacket. Yet, I long for the moment when my little charges walk through the door, toting their backpacks, disorganized flash cards, and 3,500 dried out markers.

I confessed my longing for summer to my dear friend Eunice the other day. Eunice's nest is all but empty. And there's more than a small part of her that takes delight in that fact.

"You are going to get excommunicated from the Mother's Club for talking like that," she said. "Saying that you want the school year to end is blasphemy. In fact it's just totally out there. You got a fever? Are you hormonally challenged?"

"No, I'm not hormonally challenged" I said in my defense, "but anything has to be easier than this last week has been. Take last night, for instance. My little cherubs chased me around the house with one need after another. 'Mom I need twenty bucks for the field trip.' 'Mom, I need help with my end-of-the-year projects.' and 'Mom, I'm fairly certain that the area of a trapezoid having bases 12 and 8 and a height of 5 is most definitely not 3.'

"There was a time when I hid in the back of the closet under a pile of old maternity clothes. I was just starting to feel secure when I heard the legendary, 'Mom! Mom!,' followed too quickly by, 'Oh, there you are. My science project is due tomorrow and I haven't even started it yet. I need wires, cardboard, and a few explosives. Say, and how are you with a syllabus?'"

It's more than a mother can endure.

Still, Eunice wasn't convinced that a sane mother would long for the school year to end.

"Shouldn't you be off somewhere enjoying the last few minutes of sanity that you have? Isn't there a blue light special somewhere that's calling your name?"

"But Eunice, with two kids out in the real world and the other all but raised, I'm sure you long for the days when little fingers reached up from under the table to snatch your last French fry."

"Are you crazy?" she responded with a fury. "My last kid is almost baked. In a few months I'll be able to stick the toothpick in and it'll come out clean. I'm giddy with the prospect of freedom."

"Oh, you'll miss the pitter-patter," I told her with confidence, "you know you will. The dog can imitate it, but he can't replace it. You long to share your last Diet Coke with a car full of thirsty kids. Your TV time alone is not what you always hoped it would be and although your dirty clothes hamper runs on the empty side, sometimes you find yourself looking at it out of the corner of your eye and thinking, gosh, I should have enjoyed that while it was full.

"There's a part of you, albeit small, that longs to have kids fighting over the TV set, the last popsicle, and the anticipation of sitting in the front seat. I'm quite certain there are times when you would kill to see that your precious has thrown a box of Ritz crackers, a six-pack of Go-gurt, and a box of Ding Dongs into the shopping cart when you weren't looking."

"You're right," she finally admitted. "I did so enjoy them while they were young—so cute, so sweet, and oh the hugs. I really miss the hugs."

"Then shall I put you down for a couple of afternoons with my little dears next week?"

"I said I missed the hugs," she replied firmly, "I didn't say I was out of my freedom-loving mind."

54

SVELTE FANNY IS SO OUT OF THE CLUB

I've decided that I'd be toothpick thin by now if it weren't for food. In fact, I gained five pounds yesterday simply walking past a cake. I'll admit I may have had a small sliver and was then forced to slice off another sliver in order to even up the row. Yet, I'm sure most of the weight gain occurred by simple osmosis.

With summer just around the corner, it isn't smart to have cake around the house. Cake isn't safe in the hands of a woman who can gain three pounds eating her own words. In fact, I should load up the leftovers and ship them to a house where people can eat freely and still drop a pant size.

To make matters worse, each and every advertisement this time of year asks the same thing, "Swimsuit season is rapidly approaching. Are you ready?"

Oh, I'm ready all right. I'm ready to go back into the house and spend the summer hiding under the pretense of being a busy mother—ready to hide behind the children for family photos and behind overfilled shopping carts when I'm in the store.

For the most part, I'm shaking in my boots. Already, scantily clad women are appearing everywhere—sporting the new summer lines with sun tans and shaved legs—and I've not even had time to get my knees ready.

Thank heavens, not all spring and summer events require svelte figures and firm upper arms. In fact it was quite nice the other night as the other mothers and I gathered round for our first baseball game sporting lounging garb and baggy attire.

As we unfolded our umbrella chairs and set up a nice little spot, we chatted about the usual: dirty dishes, laundry and children who became bored 20 minutes into their summer vacation. Just as we were about to sit down, I asked the inevitable, "What kind of nut designs an umbrella chair that my rear end won't fit into?"

"It's the same quack that designs waistbands that shrink an inch every season," replied one of the gals. "I have little or no chance of fitting into a one-size-fits-all line at the discount center."

"I hear ya," said another. "My husband and I have enjoyed so many rich desserts over the winter that we now have to do synchronized turning when we're in the same room together."

Then Fanny—who had been quiet up until that moment—quickly and without warning blatantly announced, "I have some good news."

Good news could mean lots of things to a thirty-something-mindset: anything from a job promotion with a personal assistant to the long-lost recipe for Aunt Agnes' peach cobbler.

"What is it?" we all asked, leaning in.

"I went shopping yesterday and you gals simply won't believe this. Turns out I'm a pant size smaller than I was just last month. And here's the kicker—I'm not even dieting."

There are times and there are places for a woman to announce she has dropped a pant size (none of which come to mind). And certainly, a ballpark, in the springtime, amidst a group of women who've been trying to get swimsuit ready since January of 1999, is most definitely NOT the time.

Dear, sweet Virginia—a gal known for her composure—replied, "Gosh girl! That is great!"

Then Hazel continued the sweet talk with, "Good for you. You are truly blessed."

But I think Esther spoke for all of us when she said, "You dropped what? You did not just say you dropped a pant size when you weren't even dieting, because if you dropped a pant size when you weren't even dieting then you should know that you are so out of the club."

Not that we had a club, but if we did have a club, then Fanny would certainly have been expelled from the club at that very moment. Nobody but nobody drops a pant size—and without trying to drop a pant size? Why, it's unheard of, unprecedented, and is more than likely illegal in most states.

"I don't know how it happened," Fanny continued. "The weight seems to be just melting off of me."

Well if that doesn't tear it.

I'm loading up the rest of that chocolate cake and bringing it to her today.

55

AND NOW, A REAL MOVING EXPERIENCE

I cannot even begin to tell you how many times I've walked through our attic and thought to myself, "Whoa! That's a lot of stuff!"

I've entertained the notion of cleaning the place out now and then, but I'd quickly resist that nasty urge and go back to more important things—like clipping my toenails.

A friend of mine actually cleaned her attic from top to bottom a couple of years ago. She'd brag at every luncheon about how she'd organized her collectibles, put her maternity garb in Rubber-maid containers, and that her seasonal decor never looked better.

I handled the conversation tactfully, but on the inside I was green with envy. My garb was out of kilter, my pretties were in disarray, and I had more attic paraphernalia than you could shake a stick at.

I determined several things then and there, not the least of which was that no one should ever befriend a woman who organizes and labels her attic.

Instead of dealing with the colossal mess, I quickly ended the friendship and decided that we'd never move. Rather, my beloved spouse and I would stay put until our final days and then let the kids deal with the attic. I even smiled when I thought about how they'd spend time in the midst of our collections. They'd sit on boxes of their old clothing and converse and reminisce as they held up one item after another asking, "What the heck were they thinking?"

I never dreamed—not even in my worst nightmare—that I would one day have to pack the attic up and move it to another place.

Then we all but outgrew our humble abode. Without warning, we had more kids than beds, more clutter than closets, and more dirty bodies than showers to bathe them.

The inevitable move to a new home loomed in the distance. Suddenly, we've found ourselves surrounded with boxes, trash, and debris. We started packing containers with a smile and wrapping dishes with ease. We packed up everything from books to socks. And yet, the whole time we knew the day was coming that we'd have to attack the attic.

We started on a cool morning with an iron-clad disposition. Armed with coffee, rubber gloves, and fashionable head covering, we marched to the front line.

My beloved spouse wasn't in the attic for more than 30-seconds before he shouted down through the access hole, "Hey, how many hibachis did you think we needed?"

"Well, one should always be prepared in case one would give out," I shouted back up at him. "It never hurts to have back-up, you know."

"That may be true, but unless you unexpectedly found yourself in the midst of the Arctic tundra with no way to grill your caribou, you could probably survive with just one hibachi."

"You're a fine one to talk," I shouted back up the attic ladder. "What sort of thought process leads to saving 17 bicycles and 36 spare tires?"

"Those parts will come in handy. You'll see."

"I doubt it. Unless, of course, you plan on giving all of the relatives a clanging kick-stand-windchime for Christmas."

"Do you really need to save this container of cardboard inserts?"

"Well, I'm not married to it, if that's what you're asking."

"And what about all of these pots and pans? You must have upwards of 12 Dutch ovens up here. Here's a box of mismatched glasses, a case of old Tupperware, and I have to wonder just how many ice chests, thermal bottles, and old coffee makers can one woman house."

"Things break down. You can't expect me to run a house without back-up items."

"What's with the fur ball garbonzo?"

"That's my grandmother's faux mink stole."

"Can't someone else house it?"

"No way! Out of all of her granddaughters, she chose me as the beneficiary."

"Man, what did you do to tick her off?"

"I helped her clean out her attic."

56

PASTA COLLAGE GOES WAY OF ALL FLESH

For the sake of love, I've become a bit overstocked on useless items. For years I absolutely adored the sentimental stuff.

I loved anything and everything that had the potential to remind me of a syrupy moment. And if it even began to resemble anything that one of my precious children's chubby hands have ever—even once in their little lives—touched? Forget about it.

I saved chunky, malformed pinch-pots, macaroni jewelry, and each and every scribble of a smiling blob in an "A" line dress with "Mommy" scrawled beneath it that they ever created.

I'm not so sure my mother was so sentimental. In fact, I still suffer mental scars from discovering that she had tossed the fun-fur ornament that I worked my cute little eight-year-old fingers to the bone to shellac for her—along with a bird's nest and my adorable gold-painted plaster-of-Paris hand print in a pie tin.

I used to think that only an ogre could toss such a thing.

I never understood her ruthlessness. Never, that is, until recently when I've had to pack up my sentimentalities and move to another home.

Just yesterday I found myself amidst a pile of sentimental debris. Rather than "ooh" and "ah" over the artistry, I asked myself, "if this pasta collage was hand made for me by a loved one, how long am I sentenced to hang on to it?"

Suddenly, instead of getting weepy as I imagined the precious hands that hand glued each noodle, I wondered if I could get it to the dumpster without getting caught.

A mood overcame me and suddenly I was tossing things with a fury. "After all," I said to myself, "shouldn't there be complex contracts involved—along with an abundance of legal representation—before a mother is required to pack up a 16-inch hand drawn portrait of Sponge Bob SquarePants? Must I display him well into my 70s? Do I owe a life-long commitment to finger painted clouds? Would life, as we now know it, come to an end if I tossed the cotton ball extravaganza of Peter Rabbit into the can?"

I think not.

Suddenly I felt liberated. I tossed out the letter people, the science projects, and enough math papers to create a great story problem (if Lori fills 16 30-gallon garbage bags a day, how much closet space will she gain in a week?)

"Wait a minute," my eldest shrieked at me as he strolled past the pile of items that were making the trip to charity. "Isn't this the piñata I made for you in the second grade? Have you really been storing it up here on the top shelf of your closet for all of these years? Far away from appreciation and the devotion it deserved?"

"Honey," I said with all of the love I could muster, "I adored this six-foot piñata. And despite the fact that it's misshapen and smells like bad Spam, I've cherished it from afar. Why, before we were forced to stow it in a box at the back of the closet, your father and I spent countless hours paying homage to it from our home office."

"I see how it is," he replied, ignoring my line of loving nonsense. "You say you love me and then you store my gift away in a place where it'll never be seen again."

"Do you want it back?"

"Are you kidding me? That thing reeks!"

I didn't stop there. As if breaking my child's heart weren't enough, I called my mother and asked if she'd mind if I took the three-foot-tall snowman that she made for me in the winter of '96 to the Bargain Bin.

"The Bargain Bin?" she screamed at me over the phone, "Are you crazy? How can you even think of giving that precious snowman to the Bargain Bin?—after all of the hours I slaved while making it for you—the painstaking stitches, the torturous hours of gluing, and the expense! Why, the cost alone set your father and me back for a week!"

"Do you want it back?"

"Oh, heavens no. But, see if I ever make anything for you again."

Yeah, she can talk as soon as she produces my plaster of Paris hand print.

57

BOREDOM DESCENDS ON SUMMER BREAK

I've decided that little boys are magnets for more boys. Little boys also attract bugs, snakes, and dirt that lingers behind the ear—but that's another column.

It's not a bad thing, not really. Boys—not unlike onion breath—tend to cancel each other out. The more little boys one has lurking about, the more they play football, talk sports, and entertain each other with sounds that would make a cultured individual cringe.

Sometimes it's so loud and chaotic, I don't even notice. Then again—despite their numbers—no group can become more bored that an assemblage of little boys.

Take yesterday for instance, when the sun was high, the breeze was calm, and the barometric pressure was at perfection. The crickets chirped, the birds answered, and Mother Nature basked in all of her summer glory.

Still I had seven boys—count 'em, seven—lying around the living room, and they were bored. Bored with a capital "B."

"What do you want to do?" asked one as he stretched back and placed his head upon his hands.

"I don't know," replied a neighbor kid with a despondent sigh, "there's never anything to do."

They were silent for a moment before one of the little guys suggested, "Wanna squirt each other with the hose?"

"Nah," a dirt-ridden individual replied, "squirting with the hose is so lame. How's about a bike ride?"

"Nah, bikes are for girls."

"My older brother rides a bike and he's not a girl."

"How's about a lemonade stand?"

"How's about cops and robbers?"

"Okay, but we get to be the robbers."

"You guys were the robbers last time. Let's do something else."

"Okay, what do you want to do?"

If one would have believed what one was hearing, there was absolutely nothing in the world for these kids to do but to sit around and watch each other outgrow their sneakers.

I on the other hand had an impossible list of things that needed to be done. The bedrooms were in shambles, the laundry was all but taking over, and we had enough dirty dishes to rival a Thanksgiving festivity.

Not to mention there were 68 pairs of sneakers in the living room alone. I decided to make up a chore list and scare the doldrums out of 'em with the prospect of hard work.

"This ought to put an end to your boredom," I said as I marched into their midst. "How about a couple of you load the dishwasher, the others can pick up the toys in the yard, and someone needs to come to the laundry room and put away the school clothes for the summer."

With that the entire group reacted with shock. It was reminiscent of the witch on the Wizard of Oz when Dorothy had the forethought to dump a pail of water on her. They didn't say, "I'm melting," but one would certainly have thought they were dissolving into the carpet.

I was trying to figure out what it was I'd said to cause such a reaction when Little Charlie said, "That's evil! Why would you even say that word?"

"What word?" I replied, oblivious to my crime.

"The 's' word," replied his buddy, Hector. "You can't just go around dropping bad words like that!"

Now, I'll be the first to admit it, I have a lot of "s" words in my repertoire. I have "shoot," for when my mother is around, "shucks," for when a priest happens by for dinner, and—when I want to get creative—"suffering succotash" always fills in nicely. Generally speaking, I save the big "s" word for special occasions, like when I'm frustrated or have dropped something really heavy on my little toe. Yet with the reactions that were on the faces of those around me, you would have thought that I had said IT—the unspeakable S-dash-dash-dash word!

After some careful reflection, I was certain. I didn't say the "s" word. In fact, I'd said nothing of the sort. "Hey," I retorted to my little band of charges, "I didn't say a bad word, I simply said school."

"No," Dennis screamed as though he were in pain, "she said it again!"

"Oh my gosh," added Lawrence. "Can you believe she actually kisses us with that mouth?"

"Well," I said with a twisted smile, "when you're out of school you can either be productive, or just sit around and think about school. After all, school is just around the corner, with school shopping and school clothes and the school supplies, why just think."

And with that I cleared the room.

You know some of the best mothering techniques are the ones you just happen upon accidentally.

58

MOVING WITH PAT

The very first time my beloved spouse moved my wares from one house to another, we weren't even married yet. In fact, we were still in the first stages of dating. That was way back when I used to go agape at his rugged, handsome looks and he still thought my knees were cute.
    Back in those days, I got by with substandard housekeeping, never gave a second thought to window washing, and often slept past ten o'clock—guilt-free. I had more dirty loads of laundry at any given time than all of the tenants in my apartment building combined. I was single, free, and content to dwell in my own squalor.
    When he offered to help me move on a Saturday, I took him up on it because I thought it would be fun. I thought that perhaps we'd load the couch and whisper sweet nothings. Then we'd toss in a couple of boxes, gaze lovingly into each other's eyes, and head off for a picnic lunch amidst the poppies.
    Imagine my surprise when I heard the doorbell ring at seven a.m. Picture my astonishment when I looked through the peephole to see him on the stoop sporting chore gloves and a horse trailer. He couldn't have looked more like a one-man moving company if he'd been sporting a t-shirt that said, "Big Bad Bob's Boxing and Vacating Service."
    "What in the world are you doing?" I asked as I rubbed my eyes and combed my hair with my fingers.
    "We're moving you today," he said as he pushed past me and inquired, "Where are the boxes?"

"I'm not quite ready yet."

"Well, let's get going! Time is of the essence. Here, I'll grab the kitchen table. You get the chairs."

He left me by the door wondering several things—not the least of which was why time would be of the essence. He started hauling with a fury—tossing in my lamps, my end tables, and my invaluable collection of aluminum glasses.

"I don't have to be out within the hour ya know," I said as he raced past me, "I actually have until the end of the month."

"Nonsense," he said as he brushed me aside and took down my hanging hook rug. "Why put off until tomorrow what one can do today?"

"Perhaps because one doesn't really want to do it all today—did you ever think of that?"

"Does the refrigerator stay or go?"

"It stays."

"What about this box that's marked 'priceless junk?'"

"That says 'priceless china' and I'll haul that if you don't mind."

"Suit yourself," he replied as he grabbed my armoire and shoved it into his horse trailer like it was a cinder block.

As he emptied the bottom floor of my apartment faster than you can say *tornado,* I headed up the stairs to change out of my bedroom slippers and into chore boots. When I opened the bedroom door I realized that I had an abundance of clothing lying about—some clean, some dirty, some items I'd never even seen before. Knowing there was no time to organize the mess, I made a big pile and then shoved it all into the walk-in closet.

The closet door wouldn't close at first. But with a little perseverance and a lot of determination fed by pure adrenaline, I shoved the clothes harder—pushed on one side, pulled on another and finally forced the door to shut.

Not wanting to take any chances, I then made a label that said, "Things to be hauled at the end of the month!" and stuck it on the door.

I was in the kitchen bubble wrapping my ceramic chickens and trying to find a box for my pens when I heard him bellow from upstairs, "Lori!"

It wasn't exactly your average summons. It wasn't one of those, "Lori, head my way when you get a chance," summons or "Lori, just the mention of your name makes me smile," that one would normally utter during courting days.

No, this was a bad "Lori." An "Ohmygosh, I didn't realize you were such a slob!" kind of summons that no woman in the midst of being courted would ever want to hear.

"Where are you?" I hollered back sweetly as I swallowed hard.

"I'm not sure," he replied. "It looks like a war zone but I think it's your closet!"

It was the first big bump in the road of our relationship—a time for me to realize that I was involved with a Bob-the-mover kind of guy who could show up with a horse trailer at any given moment. For him it was a time to realize that he was flirting around with a woman who had some serious issues with laundry.

Lucky for me, I still had cute knees.

59

IT'S NOT INSIPID,
IT'S THE SUPER HERO LOOK

When the children were smaller, I had a reoccurring nightmare that I'm sure all young mothers must have. It's the one where you're in the middle of a social function with the kids and you realize they're wearing the wrong clothes. They're adorned with swim trunks in the middle of a formal. Or, heaven forbid, sporting three piece suits at their baseball game as they slide headfirst into home plate.

I used to shudder to think.

Now it seems the nightmare has come true. The children have discovered clothing in their closets that I swear I've never before laid eyes upon. Torn T-shirts, stained shorts, and don't even get me started on the socks.

I may be overly critical of the outfits that the kids pick out for themselves. But no mother worth her salt would let a child be seen in public in green shorts and a funky bohemian T-shirt. It's a mother's responsibility to tell the children when their attire makes them look like a windsock.

It's gotten so bad that we have to have a changing session every time we leave the house. "Go and put on a different shirt!" I said to one of the boys the other day. "You look positively atrocious."

"But Mom, this is my favorite T-shirt."

"It's stained, wrinkled, and unless panhandling is on the agenda for this afternoon's events, it simply won't fit into the day."

Just then Little Charlie ran past in an outfit that looked like a combination of the Brady Bunch and Don Ho.

"Did you have a theme for your outfit today Honey?"

"Yeah," he said with pride, "check it out! These clothes make me look like Spiderman!"

How can you argue with that sort of logic? It takes a great imagination and a lot of confidence to convince yourself on a daily basis that every mismatched outfit makes you look like a super hero.

Lately, however, there's been a turn of events. It would seem that my style of dressing has become an issue for Huey, our thirteen-year-old son. I suppose I've had it coming to me all of these years. Still, I don't feel that turn around should be fair play.

After all, I don't remember the Beav ever going up to June Cleaver and saying, "Man Mom, that shirt makes you look insipid."

I blame culture and, of course, the kid's English teacher for teaching him words like "insipid."

It makes a mother feel self-conscious when her child has the audacity to say, "Mom, your shorts are too long, you look ridiculous," or "Mom, those pants make your feet look big," And what about the infamous, "Mother! What sort of thought process led up to wearing those flip-flops with those short pants?"

The other night, after a week long stint of hard work that limited my attire to work rags and paint stained running shoes, we decided to get out of the house and have some fun. I ran to the closet, giddy with joy at the prospect of being fashionable. After careful consideration and a 30-minute try on session to eliminate the fat clothes, I left the house feeling like a ten-dollar bill.

Once we got to the park, I fussed with my hair, applied some lipstick, and got out of the car feeling fine and walking tall.

Thirty seconds hadn't passed before young Huey appeared at my elbow. He was looking all around him as if he were afraid someone would notice him talking to me. "Mom," he whispered with his back to me, "why are you wearing red shorts?"

"Uh, I'm not sure," I whispered back, "but I think it's because I thought they'd look cute with my white shirt."

"Well, have you noticed that no one else is wearing red shorts?" He acted as if he was an undercover agent and I was his contact. "Look around you. You're like the only one. You could quite possibly be the only person in the whole world who is wearing red shorts right at this very moment."

"Do you want me to go into hiding?"

"I don't know. I suppose it's too late to do anything about it now." And with that, he walked away.

I could have run to the car. I could have hung my head in shame—but I decided to walk the walk and do the talk and follow in the footsteps of our eight-year-old. I may have looked ridiculous—but sometimes it's fun to convince one's self that one looks like a super hero.

60

A PERFECT PLACE
FOR AUNT PATTI'S GIFTS

I love my sister, Patti, dearly. Growing up she and I had more fun than a barrel of drunk monkeys. Together we cut teeth, ruined Barbie's hair-do, and maxed out our pretend credit cards at one imaginary white sale after another.

She's still quite the bargain shopper today and therein lies the problem. Some may remember my mentioning how she purchases presents of wretchedness for our boys at each and every turn. Her toys are ruthless, most are disgusting, and some were created to cause terror in the hearts of parents worldwide.

I'm quite certain that she does her shopping at an outlet mall next door to purgatory, in a large store that sports the name "Unthinkable Toys Are Us." Where else could one purchase a snare drum set complete with amplifiers for under 20 bucks?

Some may think me unappreciative of her generosity. These are obviously people who never saw their children open up the Stink Blaster set in its entirety on Christmas Day.

Over the past several years, Patti's gifts have caused us to suffer a great deal. There was the Sand Art Extravaganza of '97, the five-gallon bucket of Play-doh in 1998, and the Plastic Cockroach-eating Iguana that Huey received for his birthday in 1999.

I thought she'd out done herself with the alien that gave birth to a beetle via C-section in 2000, but not so. She topped that one giving them the Grand Daddy of all presents: the dreaded Chemistry Set of 2001.

There's nothing like one of those bad boys to introduce your little dears to the wild world of experimentation with polymers, acids, and bases. Not to mention the fun they can have with spontaneous combustion.

Christmas of 2004, proved to be a creative gift-giving time for Patti. Although I'm sure it's creators thought it was ingenious, my beloved spouse and I will forever remember Hair Brained Monsters as the Gia Pets from hell.

Patti has purchased for our boys bugs that come to life and reproduce after midnight. She and her husband gave them Toxic Terry's Terrestrial Junk Yard and enough jars of Ooze and Gooze to make me want to sink down deep into the sofa with a bucket of ice and a bottle of booze.

To be quite honest, I'd like it better if Patti were to stop buying gifts for the boys all together. I often tell her, "It's the thought that counts. You needn't go to all the trouble to shop and wrap and such." But she doesn't listen. Patti lives for the moments when she can pop up at a party with a sinister smile and a gift bag known as, "Aunt Patti's Whammy."

Since we just moved into a new house, Patti and Frank stopped by for a tour. "This is the living room," I said with a smile. "This is the bathroom and of course, this is the pride of all men and their kind, the furnace closet."

Following the customary "Ooo's" and "Ahh's," Patti asked with curiosity, "Say, Kid, what's that room down there with the door shut?"

I thought she'd never ask.

"Good heavens!" she exclaimed when I opened the oversized closet hidden deep within the bowels of the basement. "What sort of room is this and what on earth is that smell?"

"This," I said with a smile, "is one of the finest features of our new home. It's the heart and soul of the house. In fact, I'm sure there'll be times this room may become the very vein of our existence."

"It looks like someone set a bomb off in the middle of a noxious sand pile," said Frank as he plugged his nose.

"It does indeed," I replied with an ironclad demeanor. "You see, this is the room where the kids get to use your gifts. It's unfinished, it's raw, and with the right colors and a water supply, it could double as a bomb shelter. We've soundproofed the walls, provided a separate exhaust system, and put a Disgusting Toy Detector device here at the door to assure ourselves that your gifts can never leave the area."

"You seem as though you don't really like my gifts," Patti said with feigned surprise.

"Like them?" I replied. "It's all we can do to recover from them."

"Frank, I think we'll have to put some serious effort into our gifts from now on."

She can't scare me. I survived the Odious Odie's Oleanders Greenhouse, and the Ant Hill Indulgence that Little Charlie received for his last birthday.

Then again I'd better check. The room may not withstand Easy Earl's Earthquake Simulation System that will be new on the market this fall. That one really has me shaking in my boots.

61

DROP IN COMPANY

The funny thing about the summer months is the abundance of drop-in visitors. Funny, that is, if you're a neat freak with a dusted coffee table. But if your laundry has taken over and your mirrors lack luster, it's about as funny as an elderly aunt who stops in sporting white gloves.

Generally speaking, I take my housekeeping with a grain of salt. As the old saying goes, "If you came to see me, come on in. If you came to see the house, call and make a two-week appointment."

Or, in my case, a two-year appointment—complete with forms filled out in triplicate.

Yet, when my nephew David stopped in last week on his way home from Spain, I couldn't have been happier to see him. I simply started clearing a path through the house. I grabbed running shoes, baseball gloves, and tripped over a basketball on my way to move the laundry basket off of the couch. The kids recognized the look on my face and quickly ran to their rooms to shove the dirty clothes under their beds.

We were busily catching up on all of life's recent events when the doorbell rang again. Under normal circumstances, I couldn't have been happier to see Cousin Minnie. That is, if normal meant a cleaning service and freshly applied mascara. I gave her a hug with one arm as I shoved a dirty cereal bowl at our eight-year-old with the other.

While Minnie discussed the benefits of rhubarb jelly with David, I ducked out of the room to try and reverse the damage the state of our house may have caused to my reputation. As I was busily stashing dirty socks in our home office, I had the foresight to check the messages on the answering machine. There was the usual, "This is your Mother! Why don't you ever call me anymore?"; and the proverbial saw blade salesman calling to leave a message about a sale we simply cannot miss; and then there was THE message—the message of all messages—the message that said, "Hi Lori, this is your good and tidy friend Veronica and my handsome husband Rolley. We'll be in town on Saturday and thought we'd stop by for a visit about 6:30 or so."

"David!" I ran through the living room screaming, "what day is it?"

"Sabado."

"What?"

"Sabado is Spanish for Saturday," explained cousin Minnie.

(Because now is a good time for a lesson on the days of the week in a foreign language.)

"Today is Saturday?"

"Si."

I looked at the clock and it was 6:33. I broke into a sprint, planning to grab this and to stash that. I told the children to man their stations, gave a dust rag to Minnie, and threw an apron at David, telling him to start scrubbing dishes.

"But we're company, too," Minnie and David said in protest.

"Yeah, well, you just got bumped down to non-visitor status. Now start scrubbing pots."

We almost had a counter top cleaned when the doorbell rang. Imagine my surprise when I opened it and didn't see Veronica and her handsome Rolley as expected, but Monica, my old friend from college, and her husband Raymond.

"We would have called," explained Raymond, "but our cell phones don't get service in this state and you always said to stop in anytime."

I swiped some debris off of the couch, burnt up a batch of cheeseburgers, stuck a limp dandelion in a vase, and called it entertaining.

Entertainment it was—right up until Ralph, my husband's friend from high school, happened by. "I was in the neighborhood," he said as he handed me a bottle of wine, "so I thought I'd drop in."

"Join the crowd," I replied as I popped the cork with my teeth and then took a swig straight from the bottle. "Let me find you a place to sit down."

When Melanie, a companion from my old neighborhood, rang the bell I was ready for anything. I invited her in, gave her what was left of the wine, changed the sheets in a dirty bedroom, and apologized in advance for the condition of the latrine.

By the time Cousin Virginia showed up unannounced at 8 p.m. on her way through town, I no longer cared about the state of the house. I ushered her to a folding chair and pushed her up to the table where David was teaching Spanish to the crowd. (He had already taught the children to say filth and squalor in Spanish.)

"I can't believe you're having a dinner party and didn't let me know," said my husband as he walked in the door 30 minutes later.

"I'm sorry," I replied with sarcasm, "next time I'll call."

62

DROPPING IN ON OTHERS

Not long ago, my family and I dropped in on our good friends the Maizes. We hadn't planned to barge in uninvited, honest to gosh we hadn't. But we were in the neighborhood and we rang the bell simply because we feared they'd be looking out the window as we passed and wonder why we didn't stop in.

The fact that it was dinnertime and that the Maizes serve up the best Saturday night grub this side of the Pecos was purely coincidental, I assure you.

"You're in luck," said Roy after the customary greetings. "We were just about to grill up some cheeseburgers and we've got some roastin' ears that are just right for the pickin'."

"Roastin' ears just right for the pickin'!" Color my family happy. He wouldn't have seen a more delighted group if he'd offered up a bucket of soup bones to a group of starving dogs.

Armed with a box of salt and an abundance of butter, my family went to the table like a pack of hounds. And if it weren't for my thighs and the fact that my upper arms were sprouting bat wings, I'd have joined them. There's just something about having to stand up to lose one's stomach that makes corn and carbohydrates taboo.

The boys ranted and raved over the corn and my husband, Pat, kept nodding his head in agreement. "This corn is the best we've ever had," they exclaimed in unison. If one was to believe what one was hearing, that corn was so good they felt they'd died and gone to heaven.

"Would you like to take some home?" asked Roy's lovely wife, Egberta.

"Oh, heavens no," replied Pat, "we've infringed upon you enough."

"Nonsense," replied Roy as he headed off to get his loader, "I insist."

Ten minutes later we were driving home with the back end loaded down with enough corn on the cob, green worms, and horse flies to feed the Western Hemisphere for a month.

"What do I do with a bushel of corn?" I asked my mother the next day as I looked at the heap of produce on the kitchen counter.

"Oh, it's simple," she said matter-of-factly. "You clean it, shuck it, pluck off the nasty stuff, and then you'll want to blanch it."

"I can't believe that women still blanch in this day and age. Have we learned nothing from the women's movement?"

"Honey, you're the one who was stupid enough to bring home a bushel of corn."

I spent the better part of the afternoon removing cornhusks and that nasty hairy stuff. I toiled and I boiled and—when the time was right—I blanched each cob. By the time I was done I had enough bagged up corn to fill the freezer. It was truly blanching at its best.

I hadn't planned on serving the corn to the family right away—thinking that one does not like to just pull out the good corn for every day occasions. Good corn is sort of like Grandma's china—it has to be saved for special occasions such as Christmas, Easter, and visits from old college roommates.

Yet, I couldn't wait. So when the barometric pressure was just right, the Dow was up, and one of the kitchen counters was clean, I decided it called for a celebration with corn. With steaks and real butter, I served up the Maize's corn with all of the pride I could muster. When the family began to consume it, I sat back and awaited the praise.

"Where'd you get this corn?" Pat asked with a mouth full and a look of distaste.

"It's the corn the Maizes gave us." I replied.

"Do you still have that stuff around?"

"Stuff? You said that was the best corn you'd ever consumed."

"I was just being polite."

"But I blanched it and cut it off of the cob and everything."

"Well, you shouldn't have. That was the worst corn I ever tasted.

See if we ever barge in on the Maizes again.

63

TRIATHALONS ARE NOT MY CUP OF SWEAT

I like to exercise as much as the next gal. In fact, I'd put sit-ups right up there with a hangnail extraction, a complicated root canal, and the final stages of labor.

In hopes of getting my weight down, I have been known to walk a block or two. I've lifted green beans in the kitchen in an effort to trim down my biceps and, on more than one occasion, I've walked a flight of stairs when I could just as easily have taken an elevator ride with a shabby looking convict.

But my good friend Mabel has become a fitness queen. As I swam with her the other day, I matched her stroke for stroke for three strokes or better before I decided to work on my floating. "I have a great idea!" she exclaimed as if she'd just been hit with the best thought in the world. "I'm going to sign us up for a triathlon."

"Triathlon?" I replied as I started to sink and choked on the water. "Did you just say triathlon? As in fools who swim, bike, and run for no apparent reason? That kind of triathlon?"

"Yeah, you like to exercise. It'll be fun."

"Well, I did run the kids on errands just yesterday, but that didn't exactly turn me into Flo-Jo."

"Still, I think this would be great. We could compete together and perhaps even win a medal of some sort."

"You know Mabel," I said as I climbed out of the water and reached for my bag of red licorice, "triathlons aren't my cup of sweat. I'm more of a 'walking to the coffee pot' kind of gal and I would just as soon dust my way to fitness."

"But you could walk the four miles. No one says you have to run."

"Oh yeah? Well, what about the swimming part? Isn't there some rule in the *Marathon Guide to Self-Depreciating Individuals* that says you must be able to do an up crawl?"

"That's forward crawl, and no, there's no rule that insists you have to do great strokes. You could walk your laps. I'd even loan you my aqua boots."

"Well, there you are now. I tell ya what—how about we sign me up. I'll walk 16 laps in the pool sporting aqua shoes and a water cap so my curly locks stay fresh. When I'm done I'll throw my upper body beside the pool and wait for a couple of young, strong men to come and crane my lower end out of the water. The children can then run up to me shouting encouraging things like, 'go Mom' as the recreational choir sings out the last stanza of, "The old gray mare, she ain't what she used to be."

Mabel was nothing if not persistent. "Oh, you can swim. I've seen you."

"I faked the whole thing. I can't swim a stroke."

By the time Mabel was done, she'd tried to convince me I could float in the pool for 16 laps, skip for four miles singing "Zippity Doo Dah" and then hop aboard a scooter and zoom through the finish line sporting good posture and a smile.

I know myself better than that. I know my limitations. I'm very much aware that any fool who walks the pool would be left behind eating triathlon dust. I know full good and well the other participants would be finished with swimming and onto sprinting green pastures while I gasped for air and gave 'er my all to finish my first lap.

Eventually I'd hop aboard a bicycle and pray for an early death as the rest of the group completed the last mile on their run. The race would end, awards would be awarded, and kelp bars and soy juice would be served to the gleeful contestants.

Long after the last chub of vitamins had been consumed, long after the participants had gone home to their mud baths, long after the fans had called it a day, I would cross the finish line. There would be no celebration, no shouts of joy, and no line of onlookers waving banners as I passed. Only a janitor, pushing a broom in the parking lot, would notice me out of the corner of his eye and say to himself, "Hey, who's the fat chick?"

I shook the image from my head and said, "You know, Mabel, I think I'm simply going to have to pass on the triathlon."

"Is that your final word?"

"It is."

"Well then, perhaps you'd consider taking up Pilates with me."

"Isn't that the gosh-awful exercise class where they twist themselves into pretzels and do gut crunches as they listen to Gregorian Chants?"

"Yeah, I'll even let you borrow my exercise mat."

I gotta find some new friends.

64

NOBODY, BUT NOBODY CAN MOVE DIRT LIKE MOTHER

Following 18 grueling months of hard work and back breaking labor, we've completed enough of our new home that we can actually live in it. Although some of the woodwork isn't in place, and I'd kill for a laundry room door, it's nice to just be settled and call this place home.

Over the last months I've learned to bend rebar, drive a dump truck, set trusses, and install windows. I've also learned that whatever one charges to install wood floors—it's not enough. Although my husband feels I was made for this kind of work, it's been tough on a girly-girl such as myself.

When I finished grouting the tiles last month, I stood tall for the first time in a year. I brushed the dust off my knees and loudly announced to an empty room that I, Lori A. Clinch, had completed my last task as a construction worker. I'd nailed my last nail, bent my last length of rebar, and cut my last board. I was hanging up my hard hat and going back to being a woman who was ignorant to the world of hammers and plumb-Bobs. Manicures loomed in the distance, long lunch hours were calling my name, and I went all giddy at the prospect of spending an entire day without chore boots and kneepads.

Although my beloved spouse let me dwell in my retirement for nearly a month, he felt the need to draw me out last week to assist him with dirt work in the yard. I fought him tooth and nail. I stated my case like a lawyer with an objective. I sent petitions around the countryside defending my cause, made phone calls to the right people, and stood out in the front yard with a cup of coffee and a large sign that said, "Stop the Madness."

With all of my efforts exhausted and no avenues left to explore, I pulled out the big guns and went straight to the top.

"Say," I said to his mother as I patted her arm, "you raised this man. Surely you still have some pull. Tell him I'm done being a construction worker. Tell him that my nails are beginning to grow again and that the pit marks on my face have begun to heal. Tell him that he and his band of children can work the yard and that he doesn't need any further assistance from me. You can do that for me, can't you Mom?"

"You bet I will," she responded with a set jaw. "I'll tell him that you're a woman, and that he's put you through enough. I'll set him straight."

When Pat returned to the kitchen table, she waited for him to pull up a chair. She stared at him for a minute and then said, "Pat, Lori doesn't want to do man's work anymore. She has dishes to do."

"Nobody can move dirt like Lori can," Pat said with pride. "Besides, the kids and I kinda get a kick out of watching her work a shovel."

She didn't even argue with him. Instead of standing her ground, pounding her fist, or putting forth a single, "I mean it," she simply turned to me and said, "I've done all I can."

Prior to that day, I thought insulating the walls in sub-zero temperatures while sporting a Gortex suit and an unhappy disposition was as bad as it got. But I learned that afternoon there is nothing worse than working on the face of the sun with that man of mine. It was 358 degrees if it was a hundred and instead of taking refuge like normal people do, we were out there on the prairie pulling weeds and working the soil.

The flies swarmed about us, shade was nowhere to be found, and the grass was 3 feet tall and as dry as a burning set of chapped lips. I should have been inside. I could have been browsing brochures for a fine new collection of window treatments or surfing the net for a cute pair of Manolo Blahnicks to replace my work boots.

But no, I had to work in that heated dust bowl with the men folk.

I held out for a good 40 minutes or better before I miscalculated with the shovel and hit myself in the shin. It hurt like a monkey. I screamed and I cursed. I broke into a colorful vocabulary that included the s-word and insisted that all of the earth was a hellhole not fit for mankind. I then turned on my chapped heel and stomped towards the house.

"Do you think we've pushed her too far?" I heard my oldest son ask as I passed.

"Nah," replied my husband of many years. "Deep down she loves this kind of work."

65

BACK TO SCHOOL
SILENCE IS GOLDEN

Another school year is rapidly approaching and I'm not happy. I'll surely pay heck for admitting that. The gals in my Let's Have School Year Around Club will shun me forever. People will start to look at me differently and my mother will load me up and take me straight to her physician for a full-scale checkup. Others will surely wonder if I'm putting something besides cream in my coffee.

I didn't get melancholy about summer vacation coming to an end until just the other day when I found myself totally alone. It was a moment any normal mother would dream of. I should have donned a long robe, applied a mud mask, and run through the house doing a series of leaps and pirouettes. But instead of settling into the sofa with a box of chocolates and a good Harlequin novel, I thought about how life will be for the next nine months and I felt down right sad.

My good friend Eunice stopped by in the middle of my child-missing moment and I confessed my sadness to her. She stared at me for a second and then she grabbed me by the shoulders and insisted I look her square in the eyes.

"How can you speak such madness?" she inquired with shock. "You dare not breathe a word of this to anyone, do you hear me? They'll lock you up."

"Well doggone it," I replied, "the days went by so fast that I barely had time to enjoy the kids. We've seldom visited our favorite watering hole, we never got to lie on the lawn or look at the clouds, and we didn't even get to have a lemonade stand."

"But you hate lemonade stands," Eunice replied as she threw her hands up in disgust. "The last time you let the kids have a lemonade stand you deemed it the devil's handiwork. You said that your children were ruthless and shrewd and would surely take you for all you have when you are old."

"But what about their little signs, don't they make the cutest darn signs? And who can shout 'Lemonade, get-cher lemonade here!' any sweeter than my little boys?"

"Listen to me," Eunice said firmly. "I want you to look in the mirror and say to yourself over and over, 'I'm a good person, I'm a smart person, and doggone it, people like me.'"

When my dear friend Trixie called a while later, her reaction was much the same. "Are you out of your freedom-loving-mind?" she inquired with shock. "Aren't you tired of slamming doors, hungry kids, and the never-ending scenario of punches and jabs that are constantly followed by kids screaming your name?"

"But the kids and I didn't even get to go to a movie. We always take in at least one movie."

"That's because your older boys have moved on from the days of *Bambi* and you refused to take your eight-year-old to see *Terminator-8*."

"Still..."

"I can see the gals and I are going to have to come over for an intervention."

"But can you gals hold my hand, give me hugs, and tell me to close my eyes so you can surprise me with a bouquet of shriveled dandelions?"

"No, but we can scream loudly, knock the living daylights out of each other, and forget to flush."

Although Eunice was really worried about me, and Trixie was convinced I'd lost my last marble, I couldn't wait for my family to return home. As soon as they were all in the door, I hugged them and kissed them and told them we were heading out for one last hurrah. I gathered up lemonade and floaties and packed like mad to spend time as a family before I returned my little gifts to the world of education.

  We weren't even out of the driveway before one of the precious dears smacked his brother upside the old toboggan. Needless to say, his brother reciprocated the smack with a smack of his own. Of course, that smack was followed by another smack, screams, cries, and a plethora of name-calling that finally shocked me back into the real world.

  I turned around with wide eyes and a grimace that would have rivaled Boris Karloff. I screeched and hissed and made threats regarding life, limb, and good general accord.

  It was a good thing really. I realized in an instant that they'll be going back to school in a couple of days and that it's quite probable I'll endure the silence after all.

66

KEEPING UP WITH TOMMY'S MOM

In the fall of 1997, my eldest child entered kindergarten. It was an event to end all events. Kings have been crowned, knights have been dubbed, and presidents have been inaugurated with less fuss.

I had his hair trimmed, his teeth polished, and spent twenty grueling minutes digging the dirt out from under his fingernails. I then dressed him in crisp new duds, freshly ironed britches, and a brand new pair of sneakers. I swear, when I stepped back to take it all in, a light came down from the heavens and shone upon him as a choir of angels sang out, "Hallelujah!"

Following a celebration at McDonald's and a fashion show at Grandma's, I loaded him up and we headed off to the classroom. I took pictures, said encouraging things, and on occasion patted his head and whispered, "Mommy loves." Then I stood in the doorway and cried for the better part of two minutes. Finally, he tore his little hand away from mine and he left me with a lump in my throat and the need for a good cup of coffee and a plate of bourbon balls.

The drama repeated itself in the first and second grade, but by the time the third grade rolled around, I had so many other kids that I barely had time to complete a thought. I had a five-year-old who ate oatmeal with his fingers, a three year old who felt the need to carry 16 dinosaurs where ever he went, and a precious little four-month bundle of joy who could scream like a banshee for more than an hour.

So, on the first day of my eldest child's third-grade career, the thought of escorting him into school sounded about as conceivable as making a quest for Everest—and without a Sherpa.

"Honey," I asked as I knelt to his eye level, "do you think perhaps you are old enough to walk into school by yourself this year?"

"Nope," he responded as he tried to get his mouth around the edge of his pop tart.

"But you know that if I have to walk you in, I'll have to shower, brush my teeth, and dress your brothers in fashionable take-your-sibling-to-school outfits."

"All of the other mothers do it," he responded nonchalantly.

"But all of the other mothers don't have to pack up two younger brothers and a baby. They don't have to haul bottles, wet-wipes, diapers, and a fleet of creatures from the Mesozoic period."

"Tommy Wentworth's mom does it."

If that didn't just tear it. Tommy Wentworth's mom also volunteered for activities, dressed smartly, and drove a car without dents.

"Rather than walk you all the way into your classroom," I said as convincingly as possible, "I could simply drop you off and wait to see that you safely enter the school. Why, I'll even give you a cute little honk from the horn before I pull away from the curb."

"None of the other mothers just drop their kids off."

It was useless. I drove into the school parking lot and had barely stopped the car before my precious little third grader bolted from it and ran towards his friends (leaving behind his backpack, his school supplies, and enough Kleenex boxes to blow all the noses in Hong Kong.)

Then the baby started crying, the five-year-old removed his shoes, and the three-year-old flat out refused to budge without his king-sized Tyrannosaurus Rex.

And where, you might ask, was my I-need-you-to-walk-me-in child? I'll tell you where he was. He was no where to be found, that's where he was. I gathered the children as best I could, threw a backpack and the bag of supplies over my shoulder, and moved towards the school dragging T-Rex behind me.

By the time I reached his classroom, I was winded and cranky. The baby had gone into hysterics and my other boys had gotten into a knock down drag out fight over the dinosaur.

"Vernon," I exclaimed as I approached him at his desk. "I've been looking all over for you." He didn't say anything. Instead he rolled his eyes and looked at his buddies as if to say, "Mothers! Aren't they a handful?"

To be quite honest, I wanted to go into a full blown lecture regarding inconsiderate actions—and had I taken the time to comb my hair, I wouldn't have minded screaming and making a spectacle out of myself.

Instead I simply looked at him and asked, "Can you at least tell me good bye?"

"Oh," he replied with a flip of the hand, "see ya."

See if I ever try to be as good as Tommy Wentworth's mom ever again.

67

BLAH, BLAH, BLAH, EXPENSIVE, BLAH, BLAH

All of our appliances are in good order. I thought I should state that from the start—because when one goes through a time in her life when things break down, it usually starts with a washing machine that won't wash. This is usually followed by a dryer that won't dry, an oven that won't bake, and a refrigerator that refuses to keep anything below room temperature. But all of our appliances seem to be content and are humming along happily.

So far.

It's the vehicles that have issues. I believe our troubles first started when the air conditioning went out on my son's pickup last June. I said, "Let him live without it." It was no sweat off my nose if the kid had to ride around town with the windows down.

But the mechanic had different ideas. "Well," he said as he prepared me for the worst, "if we let the compressor remain in a state of disrepair, it will lose components. That will surely cycle back and cause another compressor to eradicate which will absolutely annihilate yet another and before you know it you'll be encountering expenses of epic proportions. Although it will be extremely expensive, I recommend that you allow us to fix it. So how are the kids doing?"

Mechanics like to bring up something stable like children after they tell you the cost of reinstating your transportation will put you in financial ruins. I didn't answer him, not right away. I was still trying to get my mind around *eradicate*. Although he said many things—and some of them were important—all I really heard was, "blah, blah, blah, expensive, blah, blah, blah, lots of money."

My knowledge of catalytic converters is also limited. So when ours went out in late July, the mechanic described my catalytic issues in great detail. "Blah, blah, blah," he said slowly and with great patience, "catalytic, blah, blah, blah, and WOW! This is going to be pricey!"

Recounting the story to my husband over dinner was quite interesting and my details were sparse at best. "How is it that you can remember nothing of the conversation but catalytic?"

"Because it sounds a little bit like Cadillac and I'm thinking one of those sounds pretty good right now."

I was handling all of the car drama for a month or two. Then the computer developed issues. For the life of me, I didn't understand it. We provided it with adequate space, dusted its surrounding areas, and made certain that its innards were properly cared for. We downloaded virus protection, provided firewalls, and kept it in a freshly decorated area in the corner of the office. By and large, it received better maintenance than the kids did.

Yet, it developed many problems, including an inability to connect with its server—like it can't live without one of those. I'm upwards of forty-years-old and have yet to utilize a server (much less connect with one.)

So I contacted my Internet provider as Windows prompted me to do. I listened to the questions the computerized system put me through, pushed buttons when asked, and wondered many things—not the least of which was, why does their computerized system get to work so well?

The Internet provider people left me on hold for the better part of twenty minutes, listening to tacky music and an occasional break through recording that whispered in a husky bedroom voice, "Your call is important to us. Our full service technical support team is doing everything possible to take your call in a timely manner." Just as The Zippity Doo Dah Band was finishing the last verse of Copacabana, I finally got to speak to a real, live human being.

I described my issues at length and responded to his inquiries. I told him my name, phone number, and—when prompted—I even disclosed my age. All of which had nothing to do with the fact that my computer's server had issues.

"So, what's your computer saying now?" the guru asked.

"It says it's feeling slightly nauseous and would kill for a good magazine and a moment to itself."

"Pardon?"

"The little box on the screen says it can't locate an IBP address. I don't suppose you have any idea what an IBP address is, do you?"

"Yes Ma'am," he responded, "your IBP address blah, blah, blah, transmits, blah, blah, blah, signals, blah, blah, blah, blah, and that's why your computer won't work."

I sure hope the washer doesn't go on the blink anytime soon. A technical dialect on agitation may be more than I can take right now.

68

SO MUCH FOR THE BOYS PROTECTING MOM

When it came to having children, I have to admit boys weren't my number one choice. In fact, when I was pregnant with my first child, I desperately thought I needed a girl. I imagined frilly dresses, pink leotards, and adorable little purses in every color. I couldn't wait to buy us matching outfits, fix us up with matching hair-dos, and I imagined the two of us baking cookies—adorned in matching aprons.

I was quite certain a little girl was just what I needed and I made sure everyone knew it. Then one day a soft-spoken woman pulled me aside and asked, "Are you sure about this girl thing?"

"Why, yes," I responded with confidence. "Can't you just see the little jewel in her first pair of heels?"

"You should have little boys," she replied. "Although they can be a handful, little boys adore their mother, bow to her every command, and should danger ever cross your path, your sons will protect you to their very death."

Well, who could argue with logic like that? I changed my way of thinking then and there. And it was a good thing too, because Batman and Rolley-Polley collections were all that the good Lord had in store for my future.

Over the past 16 years, I've watched my four boys cover themselves in mud for no apparent reason. I've seen them chase birds across the yard, throw rocks at passersby, and develop a complicated system of highways in the alley. They've played All-Star Wrestlers, ran with scissors, and did things with screwdrivers and hammers that would make the average woman hit the sauce.

On the day they learned Walmart sacks cannot double as parachutes, I comforted myself with the soft-spoken woman's words, "Boys are worth all they'll put you through because they will protect you to their very death."

So, as I worked in the yard the other night, I had no fear of snakes or reptiles. I knew my boys were nearby and if danger presented itself, I could laugh in the face of adversity. My band of young men would brave the odds, take down the opposition, and do battle with the devil himself—if necessary—to secure my safety.

After all, the soft-spoken woman had said so.

I was foolishly confident of that fact right up until the moment a killer Centipede appeared out of no where and shimmied himself across my foot.

Now, if you're not familiar with the Centipede, let me start by telling you, it is not a pleasant bug. While some will argue that it is simply a common arthropod with a billion legs that moves at the speed of light, I'm here to tell you that it is—in fact—a king-sized, flesh eating, woman-scaring varmint that would just as soon sink its poisonous jaws into your unsuspecting flesh as to look at you.

And this one was a five-inch monster!

Giving no thought to rationality, I screamed. It was not just your average scream, either. No, this was one of those blood curdling, "Oh-my-gosh I'm going to die!" kind of screams that a woman saves for moments of great anguish.

And how did my life-saving offspring respond, you might ask? Did they rush to my side? Did they sweep me away? Did they place themselves directly between me and the object of my terror and defend me to the death as the soft-spoken woman had contended?

Heck no!

They jumped five feet in the air, screamed out, "Run for your lives!" and broke into their, "every man for himself," run.

"Where are you people going?" I hollered after them.

"Is it a snake?" asked one child as he hugged his brother.

"No," I said, not taking my eyes off of the beast, "it's a Centipede and it's your God-given duty as sons to get back here and kill it for me."

"Oh, I'm not going to go anywhere near that thing," said another would be hero.

"One of you boys get back here and kill this creature, and I mean right now!" I said with my finger emphatically pointed skyward. After all, it was their right of passage, not mine.

"You go kill it," said the youngest as he nudged his sibling towards me.

"No way do I kill it, it's your turn," he replied, returning the shove.

"Nah-uh, I killed a cricket in the bathroom last week."

They stood and argued, as I—the woman they were born to protect—remained held captive in the corner of the yard. After listening to them argue over which one of them should save my life for what seemed like an hour, I took my spade and sent the dang thing to Centipede Heaven.

Just think, I put up with All-Star Wrestlers for nothing.

69

KIDS! IF IT ISN'T ONE THING, IT'S ANOTHER

I remember a time when my eldest son was always awake. Playing with his toys, excavating the kitchen floor with his tractors, and taking the bathroom cabinets apart with his 17-piece pry-bar set.

Oh, those were the days.

He never slept back then, not really. Sure, there would be an occasional yet brief nap. And of course there was a time when he was ridden with the flu and was peaceful for the better part of an hour. But by and large, he never took more than a couple of winks at any given sitting.

The first couple of months of his little life were the worst. I clearly remember rocking the little fella to sleep—looking down at his precious little face, and thinking, "My, how angelic." I'd admire his little hands, his cute little chin, and then I'd pray to God that I could get him into the crib before he woke up and started screaming again.

The process of transferring him to a place of rest was not an easy one. I'd lower him a centimeter at a time so as not to alarm him. Once his body connected with the mattress, I'd begin the painfully slow extraction of my arms. Little by little, I'd pull them out from under him. I'd even close my own eyes just in case he'd open his, making a "shh-shh" sound as I prayed he'd stay asleep.

Most of the time I never made it past the first "shh" before he woke up. But some times the gods of slumber smiled upon me. Once I even made it to the door before he woke up and started crying again.

He kept up his period of sleeplessness right through the terrible twos. And it is my contention that a more terrible two-er was never born. While other kids played with trucks, he liked the sound they made when they hit the wall. He also loved toilet paper, and what that kid couldn't do with a crayon couldn't be done. Long before he was old enough to appreciate color, he was putting it together on the wall.

His respect for literature was virtually non-existent, and while other toddlers would look at books for hours on end, mine was more enthralled with tearing out the pages. He spent the better part of his early childhood running amok. He was destroying this and into that and when he learned to ride his bike, he tore down the sidewalk with enough energy to light up the West side of the Northern Hemisphere. I had never seen such stamina.

There was never a break from his activities or a reprieve from his disasters. Because, like I said, the kid never slept.

Then my awake child turned 16. He has been unconscious ever since. He's tired when he wakes up and tired when he falls back into bed. He sleeps through the morning, naps through the afternoons, and if we left him alone, he'd hibernate right through the winter months.

On our last family vacation he slept so much we had his oxygen levels checked for deprivation. Although he woke up at a restaurant long enough to eat a triple Papa cheeseburger, he only made it half way through his French fries before he pronounced his exhaustion and headed off to the closest thing that looked like a pillow. The kid has turned into a regular sleeping beauty.

Then just yesterday it happened. Our sleeping wonder woke up. It's hard to believe, but it's true. I was on the phone and enjoying a great gossip session with my good friend Ethel, when I heard a moaning noise coming around the corner.

"What the heck is that?" asked one of my little cherubs.

"Either we're being invaded by Frankenstein, or Vernon has finally arisen," said another.

"Honey," I exclaimed as I put the phone down, "is it you? Is it really you? Are you really awake? Pat, come quickly! Vernon's awake!"

"Mmph," Vernon said through half-opened eyes. And then he spoke the first sentence he's spoken since reaching the teen years, "Man, am I beat."

"Beat? Did you just say beat? You just woke up from an extensive resting period. You don't get to be beat."

"Well, Mom," he replied as he yawned, stretched, and scratched himself, "it is now known that sleep deprivation in teenagers can lead to poor health, behavioral and attention problems in school, and we certainly wouldn't want that."

"Huh?"

"Yeah, it's true. And wow, that was quite a sentence. I'd better grab a nap."

The writing is on the wall. I may have to give that kid his 17-piece pry bar set back, and soon.

70

FALLING SHORT OF MOTHER OF THE YEAR

It hit me just last week that I may never qualify for The Mother of the Year Award. I'm also out of the running for Cook of the Century and A Wife to Die For. Since those nice folks at Desperate Housewives haven't called and requested my presence for an audition, I can only assume that it's yet another call that may never come.

But with Mother of the Year—I really thought I had a chance. I'm great at making bologna sandwiches, I possess volumes of knowledge about carpooling, and I'm all over sibling rivalry. Still it would seem that the competition is steep for Mother of the Year and one has to get up pretty early in the morning if she's going to compete against organized mamas.

And I'm simply not a "get up pretty early" kind of gal.

I like to lie in bed for the better part of the morning and enjoy a good slumber. I like the darkness, I like my jammies, and gosh darn it, I like smacking the alarm clock every ten minutes or so in order to get another good twenty winks.

That brings me to my revelation. On a dull and overcast morning just last week, I was due to arise at 7:03 am. Naturally about 7:01 am, the lump in my pillow disappeared. The blankets I'd been struggling with suddenly cascaded over me, and never before had a mattress felt more comfortable.

I did what I had to do. I knocked the alarm clock on the head for one final dose of a snooze and settled in for a nine-minute nap. Never underestimate the power of the snooze alarm.

At 7:38 I awoke to the sound of a disc jockey debating mutual funds with a caller from Wisconsin. A cute little voice inside my head told me to ignore the energy the early risers put out there and simply stay in bed. Why, I could close my eyes and pretend it didn't matter and return to the white sale I'd been dreaming about.

But that's no way to start a school day. I threw back the covers and scrambled down the hallway in a panic. "What kind of mother does this?" I asked myself as I stumbled to the children's rooms. "What maternal being worth her salt forces tardiness upon her children—leading them to a life of late appointments, missed trains, and overdue library books?"

I ran from room to room opening doors. "Kids, get up! Get out of bed."

I told myself that these things never happen to morning people—never to the organized, devoted mothers who surround me at school functions. Not to a real contender for Mother of the Year. Then I lectured me that *I* should strive to be an organized mother. I should be a systematic person. I should create a list of steps to self-improvement and make that a goal for the day.

It's what a real Mother of the Year would do.

The children did not readily stir. And why should they? They were still living in a land where a mother arrives at a dutiful hour to awake them.

"We're late," I shouted out. "Don't you understand? Your teacher is waiting, the principal is checking his watch, and all of your schoolmates who are lucky enough to have been born into a normal family are already at the school."

A couple of the kids threw back the covers and began to scurry about. One precious child—the one they call Sticky—simply opened one eye to look at me. "Wake up!" I said as I shook him. "We've no time for hesitation. You have three minutes to get out the door." Then I grabbed him by the ankles in an all out attempt to pull him from his bed as the other children ran—frantic.

"Where's my back pack?"

"Where's my lunch ticket?"

"I can't find any pants! Does no one do laundry anymore?"

"Mom, have you seen my football uniform?"

"Mom, I don't have any clean socks and I think the dog ate my shoes!"

Suddenly the guilt left me and I began to shout. I turned into a drill sergeant with a voice that would rival a blow horn. I shouted at one kid, yelled at another, and—in order to get the one they call Sticky to take an actual step towards the door—I moved in behind him and gave him a loving push.

With a spit bath or two and a quick combing of the hair, I rushed them to the car. I blew a general kiss their way, tossed in a box of cold Pop tarts, and closed the door.

Oh yeah, those Mother of the Year people should be calling any moment.

71

THERE'S MORE
TO LIFE THAN AN RX7

Although I'm basically a moral person, I have been known to fib to the children. Not big fibs, mind you. I'm honest about life threatening situations, and how much I paid for my stylish new pair of shoes. But I like to keep them on the edge when it comes to things like the reality of super heroes and where babies come from.

Most of our communications occur in the car, during long commutes to and from family gatherings, school, and each and every event that involves a ball and athletic garb. Car rides are the reason the children still believe in Santa and are convinced the tooth fairy no longer compensates for tooth loss because she declared bankruptcy and is living in a camper on a lake in Michigan.

The condition of my car doesn't matter much to me. As long as the door opens when I pull on the handle, the windows roll up and down accordingly, and the engine makes some sort of an attempt to start when I turn the key, I'm good to go.

But there was a time in my youth when I would have died for a Mazda RX7. I imagined myself in a sporty little rig that could zip me across town and corner like a dream. My hopes for acquiring an RX7 dimmed after the birth of our first-born son brought the reality that he would need more necessities for every outing than the cargo area of the RX7 allowed.

My dream of the RX7 really went to the side of the road when the second and third sons were born. And by the time the final test stick turned blue announcing the imminent birth of our fourth child, the RX7 was nothing more than a distant thought I put in the back of my mind along with gardening and world traveling.

Instead of something sporty, I'm stuck with a white suburban—a hulk of a family vehicle. I use the term *white* loosely. Actually, the paint is believed to be white but with the bugs and mud, who really knows for sure. The windows are opaque with tic-tack-toe drawn in the steam. The handles are sticky and if one were ever to discover anything remotely valuable inside my glove box, it would be an accident.

I'm doomed to cruise through town in a vehicle littered with toys, athletic devices, and dirty socks. Important papers are strewn about. The cup holders are used for little trash cans. Baseball bats, hats, gloves, and shoes are shoved under the seats.

We drive to sports practices, games, and—on occasion—to the Sports Shoppe to pick up more sports paraphernalia. As any sports fan will tell you, avid sports players can not simply show up to the field and expect to participate. Real players need nutrition—and a substantial amount of it. This requires trips to McDonald's, to Burger King, and from time to time through A & W for a Triple Papa Cheeseburger, hold the mustard and double the fries (most of which end up on the floor.)

Still, the car is the family communications center. It's where the children talk about their day, explore sibling rivalry, and—when it's done right—I get to catch up on some good gossip. On a good day last week, I learned that Tommy Jenkin's mom shops too much and that Suzy Youngman's mom does most of Suzy's homework.

I also learned that young Jack Sprat said not only the A word but also the B word, the H word, and—when he thought no one was looking—he held up a bad finger.

The chaos last Friday was the worst. One child screamed, "Look at my papers," as another said, "Charlie has foot rot and his shoes smell like bad cheese."

"Hey," said Lucas, our guest rider for the day. "I just remembered. We don't have school on Monday!" His announcement was quickly followed by a series of high five's and an abundance of cheers I felt the need to squash.

"Turns out you do," I replied with a straight face.

"We have school?" screamed Huey with disappointment.

"I hate it when they say we don't have school and then we have school!" cried Lawrence.

"Don't listen to her," replied Lucas. "She once said they were postponing Christmas vacation due to a football game and last spring she told us there would be no summer because the moon was like all messed up and stuff."

The RX7 may corner like a dream, but it could never offer me a platform for this much entertainment.

72

YET ANOTHER DARNED BUG COLLECTION

Although I'm done with my formal education and have no intention of ever again darkening a classroom door, I still have to deal with homework. Lately, I've had more lessons than you can shake a #2 pencil at. I've had to contemplate correlative expressions, create elaborate compositions, and— just the other night-—I had to get my mind around a biological equation that had me longing for soft music and a stiff drink.

They say children shouldn't have this much homework. They say a child should utilize his free minutes, address what he needs to do, and learn the discipline of good time management and study habits. Personally, I'm all for disciplining the heck out of these kids if it will spare me the details of decimals. Quite frankly, math homework gives me a headache.

And for what? I can't imagine a day in an average adult's life when she would need to know what three minus c to the third power divided by nine adds up to. I really can't.

I can balance my checkbook, compute caloric intake on my low carb diet, and manage to keep the family on a tight and stringent budget—and all without the fun of incorporating integers and common denominators into my calculations.

Don't even get me started on History. There is nothing a mother, such as myself, dreads more than the moment her teenage son plunks a fifty-pound history book (complete with maps and study guides) in her lap and suggests, "I think it's time for you and me to bond while we brush me up on the Articles of Confederation."

Doesn't that just conjure up the image of a Norman Rockwell moment?

Since it was too late to close my eyes and fake death, I braced myself and said, "Why don't you do a little stint and tell me what you have learned so far?"

"Well," he said in total seriousness, "I've learned the federalists used tough political maneuvering to win a narrow ratification of the Constitution in the key states. How much fun is that?"

I didn't exactly respond to his question and I think it was at or around the time I closed my eyes, plugged my ears, and started to hum, that he realized perhaps my constitutional knowledge was not all it's cracked up to be.

All the homework in the world pales when compared to the world of school projects.

School projects have caused more strife than any social issue known to the family unit. They have pushed American families to the brink, taken over American living rooms, and have been known to cause great discord in the hearts of God Fearing parents everywhere.

I've been tortured by Invent America, detailed solar systems, science fair experiments, leaf collections, and a 3-D castle we, as a family, erected over a holiday weekend.

Our most recent project is the dreaded bug collection. I have to say, we're up to our antennae in vermin. We've got katydids on the counters, stink beetles in the living room, and the ever-loving damselfly has all but taken over the arrangement on the coffee table. We've got ticks taped and pinned, spiders in test tubes, and if you've seen one Spotted Camel Cricket properly mounted (aka Ceuthophilus pallidus) well then, you've seen them all.

Rather than be drawn together as a family, rather than coddle one another as we join hands and learn about the wild and crazy life cycles of the Gossamer Wing butterfly, we're at each other's throats.

Meanwhile, Huey, (our young would-be entomologist who will benefit from this chaos with a grade) feels as though he's had it with the fine world of Ortopteras. Quite frankly, I fear he lacks the coping skills to survive it. Rather than enjoy his educational experience, he's been quite often shouting out, "I can't do it!"

This is echoed with sounds of woe from another brother who bellows from the great room, "For 50 bucks, can anyone tell me how many total delegates would have had to switch sides in order for all of those states to have opposed ratification?"

There's a three-second pause of silence before another child continues with a variance of either, "Gosh!" or "This is so stupid," and then we're right back to the infamous, "I can't do this!"

I think *they're* right when *they* say discipline is the key. And I'm considering a belt. What do you suppose *they* would recommend—vodka or whiskey?

73

LAUREL ALLEY IRONS

I'm not much of an iron-er—everyone knows that. I firmly believe in fabric sheets, polyester, and—when the wrinkles get tough—a quick Botox injection. Anything but an iron.
I blame my hatred of ironing on my youth. Back in my day, everything had to be pressed (including the underwear) out of fear we should have a car accident and our tidy whities would be discovered wrinkled.
God forbid.
Mother said I had a knack for ironing and therefore I was designated Head Ironer. She also said I had knacks for cleaning the windows and scrubbing the tubs. Boy was I gullible.
I maintained my status as head ironer until the Easter morning of 1976—a day which shall forever be remembered as "The Day Lori Burned a Big Iron-Shaped Hole into the Spine of Dad's New Easter Shirt."
I received a demotion that day. They all gathered around me, took my can of spray starch, looked at me in censure, and then—to show they meant business—they took the ironing board out of my room. Although Mom contended that I was still the best shower cleaner this side of the Hilton, I never again got to iron the family apparel.
Some may think it takes a lot of therapy to overcome such disappointment and most likely they are executives in stiff collared shirts. But quite frankly, being forced out of the world of ironing

was—for me—like getting an "A" on a history exam I never had to take.

From that day forward I felt liberated, happy, and free of pressed pleats and starched collars.

I met and married a man who not only tolerated un-scrubbed tubs, but would never expect me to iron his dress socks for his business briefing on Monday morning, nor his shoe strings or a silk hankie that went perfectly with his three piece suit.

And I befriended press free women the world over—females who realize there's more to life than spray starch and freshly pressed pleats. In fact, we started a support group, organized committees, and rallied together enough women with a tolerance for a disheveled look to fill a second hand clothing store.

Life went along just swimmingly. We were stepping light and moving easy in our wrinkle free cotton blends.

Then suddenly—and out of the blue—I received a phone call from Laurel, a woman who claimed to be my chum. "You'll NEVER guess what I just finished doing!" she exclaimed with great pride. "I actually used—not looked at, or found under my bed, but actually used—an IRON!" She was so proud of herself that she was ready to scream it from the laundry room, shout it from the roof tops, and contact a sportscaster to come out and do a live sideline extravaganza.

Now, I've been proud of me now and then. I've gone above and beyond, moved across the border, and have been known to take risks up to and including parallel parking, but an iron? Come on. Why would she?

"Shut up!" I replied with disgust, "You did not use an iron!"

"I did," she said without shame. "I used one. I, Laurel Alley, heated up and used an iron to do motherly tasks! I started with a Boy Scout shirt and a patch and things just went crazy from there."

"Things went crazy all right," I said as I scowled into the phone. "What were you thinking?"

"I don't know. I just took it out, plugged it in, and lost all control. One minute I was looking at a patch that needed attached and the next thing I knew I was ironing shirts, skirts, and stuff with buttons. I'm even starting to look at the bed sheets in a different way. It's all so addicting."

"Were there witnesses?" I inquired. "Could it be proven in a court of law? Is there any way you could wad up that shirt and pretend it didn't happen? If your husband catches wind of this and tells other husbands, will they—in turn—spread the word to other husbands who would eventually talk to my husband and tell him that you, Laurel Alley, used an iron? Why, the damages may be irreversible. It could only be a matter of time before my husband starts inspecting his shirts, looking through his dress pants, and coming at me with a pile of clothing saying, 'Laurel Alley irons. Why can't you?'"

I'm scratching Laurel off my list of chums and voting her out of the club for press-free women. You have to be careful with gals like Laurel. It could only be a matter of time before she lets the world know she scrubs the tubs.

74

FOR HIGH-TECH STUFF, YOU NEED A KID

My husband, Pat, goes through a technological ordeal about once a week. It generally involves something as complex as the answering machine, an alarm clock, or all of those complicated buttons on the dashboard.
"Why isn't this dang car heating up?" he asked during a cold snap just last week.
"Because you just turned up the radio, Honey," I replied with love.
"What do you mean, I just turned up the radio?"
"Well, I'm sure you meant to send a signal to the heater that you'd like some warm air, but instead you turned Britney Spears to full volume. And although some may consider her a hottie, I doubt you'll be able to feel any heat coming out of the vents simply because she's singing her 'Oops' song."
"Well, where's the button for the heat?"
"Promise to take me to dinner and I'll tell you," I said as I felt his knee.
"It's that funky little switch that says 'heater,' Dad," said our eight-year-old, Charlie, as he came to his father's rescue.
"Boy," Pat replied, "children today are ingenious, aren't they? As soon as we get home, let's get that kid to program the VCR."
Don't get me wrong. Pat is positively brilliant. He could build a replica of the Taj Mahal without consulting a manual. He can examine the structure of a building, describe the systems used, and analyze

the cost per square foot faster than you can say, "Pass me that plumb bob."

Just don't ask him to use a keyboard.

For him, "speed dial" is a quick turn of the channel knob of an old RCA TV and a "hard drive" is a trip across town with the kids. But no button-sporting piece of equipment causes him as much grief as his cell phone.

"Lori," he said to me during a phone call last week, "how do you make this thing ring?"

Ignoring the desperation in his voice, I made another attempt at romance by playing my favorite game entitled, "We're Amidst a Hot and Heavy Relationship."

"I'm not sure you should call me out of the blue like this," I said in my husky voice, "What will people think?"

Refusing to play along, he said, "They'll think you got me a cell phone that's too complicated to use."

I ignored his comment and beefed up the conversation with, "You just can't stop thinking about me, can you?"

"I can't help but think that my cell phone won't ring. All it does is shake when someone calls me."

"You mean vibrate?"

"That's what I said. The concrete plant called a minute ago and the shock of it dang near knocked me off the roof."

I knew then and there he was in no mood for romance.

"Go to the menu," I said with little or no love.

"What?"

"Go to the stinking menu."

"I don't see a menu."

"It's a small icon on the bottom of a screen."

"What in tarnation is an icon?"

"It's just a word at the bottom of the screen, do you see it?"

"If I did see it, what would I do?"

"Click on it."

"Click on it? How do I click on it?"

"I don't know. Just push the arrows around on your phone until you can click on it."

"Why do you get me these complicated things?" he retorted. "Whatever happened to rotary dials and ringing phones? Who invented a phone that sends a shock of electricity up your spine when someone tries to contact you?"

His difficulties with car heaters and cell phones are only the beginning of his technological problems. He can't set an alarm clock, refuses to operate the microwave oven, and you should have seen him try to tackle the remote for our new digital TV.

Last night he gave up all hope and again requested the assistance of his youngest son. "Dad," said the darling little eight-year-old, "this is so easy. All you do is go to *guide*, like this. Then you hit *select*. Then you scroll through the stuff until you find your category. Then you scroll through the channels like this until you come to the channel you want to watch. Then you hit the orange button."

When I happened upon Pat later, the remote had been tossed aside. His arms were crossed firmly across his chest. He had a scowl on his face and he was staring at a channel that was hopelessly playing, *Sleepless in Seattle*.

I may get him to be romantic yet.

75

BUSTED OVER
A DIRTY PAIR OF SOCKS

Children enjoy nothing more than a crisp, clean pair of white socks—properly sized foot wear with a reinforced heel and a custom fit toe. Throw in a snug fit, and a band that's just barely visible above the ankle, and the kids will feel as if their feet have died and gone to heaven.

My children rarely experience footwear bliss and I'd like to formally state for the record this is not my fault. I attempt to collect their socks, heaven knows I do. I've pulled dirty socks out of gym bags, sand boxes, and the gas tanks of their Little Tikes Cozy Coupe cars. I've soaked them, I've scrubbed them, and I sent them through the dryer sporting the mountain fresh scent of name brand bleach.

Sometimes the socks are paired and actually returned to a drawer to await further use. Sometimes they hang out in the dryer for a number of cycles waiting for a person or persons who feel like assisting with the mating process. But more often than not, the socks are tossed into a basket with other unmated socks to spend the indefinite period of time they will one day refer to as their lonely years.

Either way, my children have access to clean socks and I feel this information should be made known—especially since I've not been able to live down what happened in an all-school Mass that occurred in 2001.

At or about the time this Mass was being held, I was home enjoying a lovely lunch. Meanwhile, the priest, Fr. Richard, was beginning his sermon.

The church was packed with the Catholic school system in its entirety. Teachers and students were in attendance, principals lurked about, and members of administration were seated front and center.

Fr. Richard began his sermon with a punch. "Clean socks are a good thing," he stated for all in attendance. "My mother liked clean socks, I like clean socks, and you," he said to a young parishioner in the congregation, "do you like clean socks?"

"I do like clean socks," replied the little guy.

"That's good to know," continued Fr. Richard. "Tell me, Son, are your socks clean?"

They say there was a shuffling and that the cute little 1st grader actually stirred in his seat with discomfort. That's what they say, but I couldn't prove it because, you see, I was having a salad at the time and living under the false pretense that all was right in the world.

"No," the 1st grader finally answered.

"Your socks aren't clean?"

"No, Fr. Richard, they're not clean."

"Were they clean yesterday?"

"No."

"The day before?"

"No."

"Tell me, Son, how many days are you into these socks?"

"Three."

Instead of moving past the informant and his tattle tale information and getting on with his homily, Fr. Richard stepped closer to the student with his microphone in tow, "You're three days into your socks?"

"Yes, Sir, I am."

"Tell me, Son," the priest asked for all to hear, "who's your mother?"

I imagine at this precise moment, one could have heard a pin drop. In fact, I'm quite certain that one could have heard a butterfly flap its wings outside the windows and a baby cry in China. It's rumored that any and all parishioners in attendance leaned forward in anticipation of the answer, which—of course—my young Huey proudly gave. "My mother is Lori Clinch."

I'm glad I wasn't there. It was not exactly my shining moment. I remained blissfully oblivious for the better part of the day. I wasn't suspicious when the principal looked at me later that afternoon and then hung his head in shame. I never gave a second thought to the janitor's "tsk, tsk" as he passed. In fact, it wasn't until that evening I learned about my new "fame" when my good friend Ethel called me and said through a bout of laughter, "Boy, did Huey drop the bomb on you today. You don't have clean socks at your house and now—thanks to the morning Mass—the whole world knows it."

I felt I was the only mother who fell short in the sock department and I've felt that way for the past several years—right up until just last week when I was at the school and helping to weigh a darling little group of shoeless 1st graders.

"Say," I said to one little lad as he climbed up on the scale, "you only have one sock."

"I know," he said with pride.

"So, where's the other one?"

"This sock is the only sock my mom had clean."

I don't know who she is, but I'll tell you this, that little guy's mother is my kind of woman.

76

WHAT WAS THAT KID'S NAME AGAIN?

Turning 40 has had some real adverse effects on me. My face shifts when I smile, my dimples are no longer cute, and try though I may, I can't lose a pound to save my soul.

Still, I don't mind so much what age has done to my body. It's the mush that the years have left me for brains that's really getting me down—and I'm getting worse all of the time.

I've often admired people with a good and solid memory. There's nothing more impressive than a person who can remember dates, places, and local events—people who are always aware of who they are, where they're going, and what they're going to do when they get there. I feel such people deserve applause, praise, and perhaps a curt smack upside the head.

I'm especially jealous of the individuals who can remember names. They simply make the rest of us look bad. My good friend Eunice, for example, is a real brainiac who can remember the identity of every person she has ever met. "How do you do that?" I asked her the other day after she greeted several passersby by name.

"It's all in the vault," she replied, tapping her head.

That's a tough pill to swallow for a gal, such as myself, who's been known to refer to her own children as, "little What's-His-Face."

While some people seem to get smarter every day, I seem to lose 100,000 brain cells every time I turn around. My lack of brilliance affects me at least once daily, and sometimes twice on the weekends. For instance, I distinctly remember an incident just last Saturday—although it could have been in July—when the phone rang and a woman asked, "Lori, did you forget me?"

"That depends," I replied with concern. "Who are you?

"Lori!" she said with frustration, "It's your mother! I've been waiting for you to get back to me all afternoon."

"Oh yeah, Mother. Gosh, I'm so sorry. It's just been crazy. The kids have been running amok, the refrigerator won't make ice, and I'll be danged if the dryer didn't pick this precise moment to take up smoking. By the way," I asked before she hung up on me, "Who did you say you were again?"

Lack of elasticity and brain cells aren't the only ill effects I suffer from aging. For one thing, I've noticed that rest has never been more important to me. I like to sleep until the very last minute available and then hit the snooze button and cozy-in for another 10 minutes. It's a flaw that's worsening as I age—and if I'm ever on the market for resale, I'll do my best to change it.

Needless to say, early morning activities aren't exactly my strong suit. So when the phone rang this morning at 7:56 AM, I wasn't exactly in the midst of my calisthenics and early morning devotions. The way I saw it, I had 4 minutes to sit in the chair and stare, and it was going to take more than some morning person on caffeine to get me motivated.

"Good morning, Lori," said the school secretary with enough early morning chipper-ness to be envied. "How are you today?"

Sunrise phone calls from school are never a good thing. They only call when clothes are soiled, or when little Johnny's presence has been requested at the principal's office for the 3rd time this week. And normally the really early morning phone call means precious little Lawrence just upchucked and immediate retrieval has become necessary.

"Do you have a sick child, JoJo?" I asked without further adieu.

"Yes I do."

"Oh, man!" I replied as I mentally felt my plans for the day fall like a stack of cards. "Which one?"

"Matthew is sick."

"Shoot, that darn kid. I could have sworn he felt fine this morning. He looked good, smiled when asked, and I'm quite certain he put down more than his fair share of Pop Tarts."

As I gave JoJo my line of reasoning, I tried to picture young Matthew. Did he have auburn hair and big blue eyes? Was he that cute little blonde, or was he the toad collector who made homes for every animal that hopped into the yard?

"JoJo," I finally responded.

"Yes Lori."

"I don't think I have a child named Matthew."

"Oh, you don't. Matthew is mine."

"Then why are you calling me?"

"To remind you that you are down for recess duty."

"But you said I had a sick child."

"No, you asked *me* if *I* had a sick child and I said 'Matthew is sick.' I wondered how you knew."

They may have me committed any day now.

77

A VICIOUS CYCLE
AT THE DOCTOR'S OFFICE

"I'll make a deal with you," I said to my husband as he fired up the BBQ for an outdoor cookout. "How about if you go in for an annual physical, and then I'll go in for mine."

"I went first last time," he said without so much as looking up from the burgers.

"Nuh-uh," I replied, "I went first in '95 and you went first in '96 and that makes this the year that you have to go first".

"What about '97?" he asked, as he spritzed the fire and peered at me from above the grill.

"I had a baby in '97, which caused a serious topsy-turnsey, clearly making any and all deals concerning complete physicals null and void. That makes all of the even years mine and the odd years yours to have the first physical."

He gave me some line about being busy and I gave him a line about early diagnosis. He then told me that physicals are humiliating and I went on to describe the final stages of labor. I was making a pretty good case until he offered to do the dishes. I give in to almost anything when he offers to do the dishes.

There was a time back in the '90's when I saw our family physician more than I saw my own mother. I had him on speed dial, had access to his party line, his cell number, and when the nurses announced that Lori needed to see him right away, our doctor never once asked, "Lori who?"

Thankfully, times have changed. The children's sinuses have cleared, their eardrums have dried up, and most of the virulent viral infections have come and gone.

In fact, when I waltzed into my doctor's office the other day, I hardly recognized a face (including the darling face of the young nurse who called my name and then asked me to—and I quote—"Hop up on the scale.")

Anyone who knows me knows that I don't like nurses who ask me to hop up on the scale. I just don't see the sense in it. I feel that unless I appear to be toting 30 gallons of water on my body and making a sloshing sound as I saunter across the floor, my weight is no one's business but my own.

But I was in a good mood that day. I assured myself that my scale at home was way more accurate than their deranged scale that likes to add 20 pounds to any and all individuals forced to be exposed to its numbers.

The nurse wrote down my weight and told me to go into room number four. She sat across from me, flipped through the pages in my chart for a minute—then she clicked her pen a couple of times and inquired, "So, are you still cycling?"

I sat for a minute and looked at her. I turned my head slightly to the right, pondered her question, then pondered some more and finally, with as much brilliance as possible, I mumbled, "Huh?"

She leaned in, spoke a little slower and a little louder, and repeated her question without hesitation, "Are you still cycling?"

"No," I finally replied, "the kids and I had to give that up once we moved to the country."

Then it was her turn to look at me with a query.

We stared at each other for what seemed like

an eternity—me, wondering why she didn't understand my answer, and she wondering if I'd lost my mind somewhere between the scale and room number four.

"Well," I finally explained, "we had to quit cycling. We just didn't have a choice—what with the dirt roads and all."

There was another awkward moment of silence as I sat there amazed that she knew I rode a bike in the first place—and I'm sure she had all sorts of thought processes running around in her brain as to why I had to stop "cycling" after I moved to the country and why my kids were involved.

After she explained her question better and I finally got the gist of what she was trying to ask me, I not only felt stupid, I felt really old. I looked at her and asked, "Should I not be cycling at 41?"

"Well..."

"Cuz you know," I continued defensively, "not only am I still cycling, but most of the women that I know are still cycling. In fact, all of my closest friends still cycle. I dare say we all cycle all of the dang time. For that matter, we may cycle for the better part of the next week."

Am I still cycling? The nerve!

I can't wait to hear what sort of fun question she has for my husband.

78

PAPRIKA MAKES UP FOR WHAT MEALS LACK

"Oh no!" exclaimed our eldest offspring as he came into the kitchen the other day. "Mom's been messing with the paprika."

"Why would she get into the paprika?" questioned Huey.

"Has she been watching the Family Experimentation Channel again?" asked Lawrence as he joined the group.

"It's nothing that simple," commented their father from a dark corner of the kitchen. "Your mother made me go to the doctor and he said my cholesterol is above average. I made the mistake of mentioning it to her and now *she's* decided to put me on a low fat, no taste, high vegetable diet—and you know what that means?"

"Yeah," said the eldest, "that means what her meals lack in taste and texture, she'll make up for with paprika."

The thing about men is they just don't appreciate what we women go through to keep them alive and healthy. Why, if it weren't for me, my beloved would be sitting in a lodge somewhere eating deep fat fried onion rings with a side of real mayonnaise.

I shudder to think.

When my husband first learned of his elevated cholesterol level, he was determined to do something about it. He was totally gung-ho, a real Captain Ima Lowcholesterol. He read the labels, refused to eat anything that wasn't on his list from the doctor, and feared anything that tasted good would elevate his LDL.

I was impressed by his enthusiasm to make a change in his lifestyle. Out of love and adoration, I single handily created a lovely menu for him that consisted of faux-cheese, faux-ice cream, and my own personal favorite, faux-bacon strips.

Things went splendidly until last Wednesday. With his head down and a scowl on his face, my husband quietly sat down for lunch and ate his whole-wheat turkey and sprout sandwich, light on the spread, heavy on the mustard. He complained that the cauliflower had no zest and wondered out loud what low fat people eat for dessert.

On Thursday, he returned from work and announced that his co-workers had contended that—and I quote—"If you can't eat what you want, then life ain't worth the living."

"Therefore," my precious husband went on to say—with his chest puffed out all cute and everything—"I'm going back to eating like a normal human being."

How darling is that?

To celebrate the moment I whipped him up a stellar batch of low fat chili. I was sure he'd be impressed. I thought he'd pat me on the back, boast of his love for his bride, and offer up a toast with a glass of skim milk.

Instead, as he looked into his chili bowl he grumbled, "Where's the beef?"

"There's meat in there," I said as I counted out his daily serving of saltine crackers.

"I don't see the beef."

"See," I responded as I held the bowl up to the light, "look right here. Don't you see it? That there's hamburger."

"I don't see the hamburger," he said. "All I see are beans and I swear there's enough of 'em in here for an army."

"You're just lucky I didn't make it with fish," I said in my defense.

He wasn't so quick to respond to that. He just stared at me with wild eyes and amazement. He looked like a deer caught in the headlights. "You'd really put fish with beans?" he finally replied as if the thought of it were sacrilegious.

"Happens all of the time."

He took a deep breath, put his hand to his mouth, and gasped, "Does your mother know?"

"You can whine like a two-year-old," I said, ignoring his dramatics, "but you ain't going off this diet. I'll be danged if I'm going to be a 40-something widow who's raising the kids on my own because my stubborn husband can't eat a bowl of low fat chili."

"I'm still hungry," he proclaimed after he gagged some down.

"Says here you can have a half of a banana," replied one of the boys, as he brought a food chart over to the table.

"Who eats a half of a banana?" he protested.

"People who want to live," I pointed out.

"What are you going to do with the other half? Put it in the fruit bowl in hopes some desperate soul will happen by and consume the other half? Do you really think someone is going to come along and say, "Boy! That half of a banana looks good. Let me just cut the black mushy end off that bad boy and consume it like nobody's business?"

"Actually, yes. I think it's bound to happen."

And you know, with a little paprika it didn't taste too bad.

79

POSSUM REMEDY ISN'T FOR FAINT OF HEART

I suppose I should defend myself regarding the advice I gave Greg Bean, an editor from New Jersey, who wanted to rid his garage of a possum. After all, I certainly wouldn't want people thinking I don't adore God's little creatures.

I must say one would be hard pressed to find an individual who loves animals more than I do and the proof is all around me. I have a dog. I have several cats and, on any given occasion, one could easily find a turtle, snake, or overzealous frog in various containers in my children's bedrooms.

Quite frankly, I should be up for some kind of award.

My Grandpa Stubbs was a hillbilly from the Ozarks who knew all about small critters and their ways. He had ways to rid the residence of any sort of varmint imaginable. Grandpa knew how to raise 'em, how to kill 'em and which ones made for the best eatin'.

It's quite a lineage for a gal such as myself—especially since I am not fond of rats, ferrets, or anything that sports a long tail and beady eyes.

So when good old Greg Bean e-mailed me and told me that a possum took up residence in his garage and that he was desperate to be rid of it, I simply offered up Grandpa Stubbs' old family recipe. "Better hurry," I concluded, "he could be a she and she could have taken up with a neighboring possum, if you know what I mean. You'd hate to have the whole famdamily moving in."

Naturally, I had a good chuckle at his expense. But possums are funny—especially when they're in someone else's garage.

Greg e-mailed me back with, "What if he dies in the insulation between the walls?"

"Your possum may quite possibly die in the insulation," I admitted. "But I ask you, what's going to keep him from meeting his maker between the walls anyway? He could be overcome with possum flu at any given moment. He could catch his death of pneumonia. His little ticker may suddenly become diseased and the next thing you know he'll be heading for the insulation with angina. I say give him a little push with my old family recipe. At least you'll have the satisfaction of letting him know who's the real boss of your garage!"

It was sound advice if ever there were any. It was painless. It was clean. It simply screamed, "Rodent Free Environment."

Greg not only had my idea to work with, but he'd received lots of friendly advice from faithful readers on the East Coast—including the woman who was outraged when Greg said he'd like to catch the possum and let him go in the park. She feared the possum wouldn't speak the same language commonly shared by the other possums in the park.

At least my recipe offered some sound solutions to rid his garage of possums. And did he thank me? Did he applaud my efforts? Heck no!

Rather than commending me for my ingenious plan, he wrote a column that warned my husband to fear my wrath and the general public to steer clear of my cooking if I was the least bit infuriated.

I must say, that was a fine how do you do. A family—such as mine—risks life and limb to experiment with rodent control and then passes on a wealth of knowledge to desperate victims such as Greg Bean and this, THIS, is the thanks we get?

Oh, just you wait. It won't be long. Locusts may creep up. Vermin could seep in. His property could be overrun with snakes and reptiles, and who—I ask you—who will be there to offer advice for pest control? Not good old Lori Clinch, that's for sure.

If he gets cockroaches, he's on his own. Head lice, I'll look the other way. If one day he gazes out in the yard and sees that the possum indeed spoke park possum language and invited not one but several of the "guys" back for a beer at the Old Bean's Garage and Diner, he needn't call me. For I, Lori A. Clinch, will no longer offer up my knowledge and wisdom at his beck and call.

Why, he'll rue the day.

He e-mailed me last week and said he had a skunk lurking about his favorite tree. It seemed to have set up residence. What to do? Grandpa Stubbs' had an old family recipe that would have skunks packing up shop and heading for the high country faster than you could ask, "What's that smell?"

But I ain't sharing.

80

NO MISTAKING WHO THAT KID WAS

Is there anything in the world more precious than a smartly outfitted child sporting freshly pressed pants, polished sneakers, and a look that is topped off with a crisp, neatly trimmed hairdo?

As everyone knows, behind every handsomely dressed child is a woman with fashion sense. Behind every baseball player in a bleached uniform is a gal who knows how to run the laundry, and behind every kid with slicked down hair, parted neatly down the side, is a gal with a comb.

It reflects greatly on mothers such as myself—you see, wherever the children are, wherever they go, whatever they are doing, if their appearance is bad, people don't look at them and inquire, "What was his father thinking?"

This is true even if the child is accompanied by the father and the father alone. Instead, the general population looks at a shabbily dressed youth in mismatched plaids and polka dotted shirt and wonders out loud, "Where on earth is that child's mother?"

To further complicate the matter, men don't notice when a child is mismatched. It's just not in their genetic code. They don't notice dirty faces, runny noses, or little hands sporting enough filth to contaminate the Western Hemisphere. Rub some gum on a kid's cheeks, roll him in the mud, walk him through a lumberyard, and women and men alike will look at him and ask one another, "What sort of mother…?"

Which brings us to the case in point: On a recent Friday night, our darling child Lawrence was asked to spend the night with a nice and upstanding family in the community—the sort of family everyone knows and people tend to look up to.

I'd packed Lawrence for the night with haste—I must admit that—but it's hard for a woman to adorn her children in the middle of the Christmas season. I had bells to jingle, halls to deck, and I'll be danged if that Christmas tree was going to rock around itself.

A better mother would have fashionably coordinated. She would have matched the socks with the shoes, opted for the name brand sweatshirt, and—when push came to shove—she would have taken the time to freshly press the family crest.

As for me, I impressed myself with my ability to remember clean socks and a toothbrush.

When the father—the head of the nice and upstanding family—called bright and early the next morning to see if I minded if Lawrence accompanied him and his son to breakfast, I responded with, "Shoot, no! Have a good time."

And when the happy father called an hour or so later to see if Lawrence might tag along on some errands that included a lumberyard and Wal-mart, I never—not once for a second—thought to ask about Lawrence's appearance. After all, I'd packed his clothes myself, hadn't I?

Several other phone calls followed that included lunch at a busy restaurant, a basketball game that was well attended by the bulk of the state of Nebraska, and say, while we're at it, "I think I'll take the boys to an over-crowded movie."

It goes without saying, most of the city's population had been exposed to young Lawrence and—thanks to the stop they made at the local feed store—some of the fine folks from up north.

I had no problem with it. In my mind Lawrence was enjoying himself a fine day on the town while I stayed home listening to voices singing "let's be jolly, deck the halls with boughs of holly." In fact, I was fine up until the moment Lawrence walked through the door sporting an all day sucker, uncombed hair, a dirty face, and his younger brother's four-sizes-too-small Jethro Clampett pants. They were bright, tight, and hit him mid-calf like a pair of badly fitted capris.

"Honey," I exclaimed as he walked through the door, "what on earth are you wearing?"

"I'm not sure," he replied between licks, "but I think you gave me Little Charlie's pants."

Maybe no one saw him, I thought to myself, maybe he moved through crowds unnoticed—or better yet—perhaps everyone thought Lawrence was a member of the nice and upstanding family—perhaps a third cousin from Hickville, twice removed.

When Lawrence walked away with a shrug and a smile I noticed the back of his sweatshirt. Not just any sweatshirt, mind you, but his favorite sweatshirt—the one that fits nicely over t-shirts and jerseys, sports grass stains on the elbows like a badge of honor and has "CLINCH" printed proudly in bright bold letters across the back.

I suppose it could have been worse. Lawrence could have cared.

81

LOOKING FORWARD TO THE CHRISTMAS WEE HOURS

It's Christmas time, and for me the season officially arrived the second I heard that dang dog barking out Jingle Bells on the radio. Oh, the unadulterated bliss!

The big day is just around the corner and I'm taking every short cut available to me. I'm re-gifting last year's fruitcake, I've let nature trim the house, and with a little luck the Christmas tree will snow on itself.

The smartest thing I did was to cut out the Christmas baking. My defense is I'm thinking of my family's health. It seems to be working splendidly despite the fact that one of the children is standing in the kitchen dressed as a bowl of lettuce and holding a handmade sign that reads, "HIGH CHOLESTEROL TESTS ARE THE WORK OF THE DEVIL." I couldn't swear to it in a court of law, but I'm fairly certain the handwriting is his father's.

Gift exchanging seems to be on everyone's mind. Even my handsome and loving spouse seems to be tossing it around. "What would you like for Christmas this year?" he asked me as he balanced the checkbook. My mind raced as I thought of candlelight and little boxes and the commercial where a wife steps out into a clean garage sporting fresh makeup and silk jammies as her husband surprises her with a new car.

I was about to plant a kiss on my beloved spouse and blurt out a list when he said, "And let's not forget the new fuel pump we just installed on your suburban."

My guess is we won't be having a diamond moment under the mistletoe this year. Yet I'll not complain. It turns out the gifts I give may not be much better. In fact, my family has reported when it comes to giving presents, I am the world's worst. In my defense, that Salad Shooter was a great price and you have to know it was appreciated when their crayon sharpener bit the dust.

Last year I took advantage of every Christmas sale. I swept up the clearance racks, stocked up on memo pads, and was thrilled when I discovered red pillowcases for the children's beds were being offered at bargain basement prices.

I also kept in mind that they wanted a CD, an MP3, and one child even asked for a portable CD with an MP3 that can play anything downloaded from the old PC. I even had a child who requested a DVD that's both AC and DC.

Would anyone care to buy a vowel?

I purchased with a vengeance, wrapped with a smile, and crawled into bed on Christmas Eve with visions of microchips dancing in my head.

I could barely wait for the children to get up. I've always been crazy about the Christmas morning pitter patter and the giggling that can be heard around the tree long before dawn, as the kids realize that Santa came.

Dark and early on the Christmas morning of 2005, somewhere between the hours of three and five a.m., I awoke to a precious face and a large pair of eyes that were extremely close to mine. "Mom," the precious face whispered, "Mom, can Little Charlie and I open a present?"

"What time is it?" I asked as I was being pulled into the moment.

"It's Christmas time!" they exclaimed as they

scampered away. I smiled despite myself. In my mind's eye, I saw them under the tree searching for the perfect gift to open. A new controller for their PS-2, a new CD, or—if they played their card's right—they could very well be out there pulling out the MP3 with great hopes it'll also play their DVDs.

When I heard them come back into the room, I was so excited I could barely contain myself. They stood at the foot of the bed tearing open the packages with frenzy.

"Pillowcases?" Little Charlie exclaimed into the night. "You bought me pillow cases?"

"What kind of thought process leads up to buying pillow cases for a kid?" echoed his older brother as he opened his very own set.

"You bought the boys pillow cases?" inquired my husband who had been sawing logs up until that moment. "What'd you get me— guest towels?"

And that concludes the memories of Christmas, 2005. When they reflect on Christmases past— and you know they will—the little ingrates will always remember 2005 as the year the old gal tried to buy them off with pillowcases.

I can barely wait until the wee hours of Christmas, 2006, when they awake to discover that dear old Mommy bought them the flat sheets that match.

82

HOW I SCARED
THE BURGLAR AWAY

When the doorbell rang last Tuesday I wasn't too alarmed. Then I saw a stranger through the glass and the rational voice that I often hear inside my head told me, "DON'T OPEN THAT DOOR!"

Naturally, this is the same utterance that also tells me I should NOT purchase gifts for myself just because they're 75 percent off—and I've been known to ignore that voice.

So I opened the door. The man didn't seem too threatening at the time and simply wanted to know if I knew where the Hodges lived. I told him I didn't and shut the door.

The situation bothered me, but I didn't know why. Some might think it was his demeanor, others would suspect it was his shifty eyes, but I believe it was a woman's intuition. Now that I think about it, it could have been the hockey mask that was hanging out of his back pocket.

(Kidding, just making sure you were paying attention.)

He left and I made lunch for my husband. Pat came home and dined and then left as I commenced to prepare for an afternoon of Christmas shopping.

I went into the garage to get some stuff out of the car when I noticed that the garage walk door was unlocked. The voice inside my head again spoke and told me to lock that door.

I'm pretty sure this time the voice was God, Himself, because the voice wasn't cute. Rather it was one of those, "And I mean it!" voices. Any individual of sound mind and body listens to that voice. So I locked the door and walked towards my car. Then I heard a vehicle come speeding into the driveway.

I went into the house and looked out the window and I'll be dogged if that same man wasn't right smack dab on the front porch.

Well-ell! I certainly wasn't about to open the door this time and I certainly did NOT need the little voice inside my head to tell me it wasn't a good idea. After all, if I didn't know where the Hodges lived at 11:30, then I certainly did NOT know where they lived at 12:45.

The guy rang the bell with a vengeance and finally walked off the porch. It would have been a great relief if he had left. But he didn't, and I'd barely had a chance to cross the foyer when I saw his reflection in the mirror. I'll be dogged if he wasn't coming back up to the door. I went into the kitchen and grabbed the portable phone, my cell phone, and a phone book (might as well call Penney's to see if they could hold their sale prices until 3, what with the burglar and all.)

When I again worked up the nerve to peek around the corner he was gone. He had not, however, headed off to torment others. Rather, that nasty creep was busily trying to pick the lock on the garage door—the very door I had just locked.

Now, I'm not one to lose composure. However, I was a little beside myself. My heart was racing, my knees were weak, and I'll be danged if I could unclench my fists long enough to use the phone.

Somehow, I managed to call the neighbors in hopes they could come and rescue me. I was in the middle of leaving a frantic message on their machine when that guy again appeared at the front door. He gave it one desperate, final ring before he finally got into his car and drove away.

Now, I think we can all attest to the fact that a would-be burglar leaving the premises is always grand. But wouldn't you know it, that dirty would-be thief did a u-turn and headed down a road that leads around to the backside of the house.

So NOW I call the law (I'll say it for you—DUH!) The dispatcher asked me to stay on the line no matter what—which was not a problem because I don't think my fingers could work well enough to push the hang up button anyway. I was busily answering her questions when I heard a noise in the basement.

(Kinda makes your blood run cold, doesn't it?)

I scurried to the kitchen and looked out the all-glass door (can't have enough of those) and down onto the patio below and I'll be danged if that abominable man wasn't busily trying to break into the mud room with a screwdriver.

Color me moving from scared witless to just plain mad. After all, THAT'S A NEW DOOR! I banged on the window with a vengeance, and screamed out objections. Much to the dismay of my mother, I did say the "d" word—but gosh darn it, you show me someone who wouldn't curse at this point and I'll show you someone who's not attached to that door.

Just then this would be burglar turned and looked at me as if I were insane. He then shrugged his shoulders, shook his head as if to say, "Women!" and he turned and walked away,

And that, my dear friend, is how I scared off the burglar. A long interview and a photo line-up led to an arrest of a man who was a suspect for a whole rash of robberies. Hopefully he'll be spending a great deal of time sitting in a jail cell contemplating what he did wrong.

If I weren't so busy trying to finish up my Christmas shopping, I'd go down there and educate him.

83

FLU BUG COMES HOME FOR THE HOLIDAYS

Even though we knew others were suffering through the flu season, we Clinches had been getting along just swimmingly. We avoided the sick, kept our distance from sniffle-toting children, and applied antibacterial lotion at every turn

We'd heard tales of woe from parents regarding late nights and doctor visits. And—since we are a good and decent people—we offered sympathy from afar as we shamefully prayed, "Spare us, oh Lord."

We made it through unscathed up until the other morning. As the other children were racing down the hallway, busy about their day, there was one who staggered behind. It always scares me when one staggers behind. He appeared weak, fragile, and (sadly enough), he was the color of a chunk of provolone cheese.

"I'm sick, Mom," he said barely above a whisper, "real sick. My head hurts, my nose is plugged, and if I never have to swallow again, it'll be too soon."

With Christmas day rapidly approaching, I was left with no choice but to take action. My mind played several scenes in my head up to and including the Christmas of 2003, when the flu ran rampant throughout the abode, leaving no stomach unturned.

So, while a better mother would have rushed to this sick child's side, taken his temperature, and quickly shoved a Vick's vaporizing plug-in into the nearest receptacle, I reacted more like an experienced parent with errands to run and a season to put on.

I quickly placed an invisible shield around him. Then I shoved the healthy children behind me and scooted a can of disinfectant at him. "Here, Honey," I said with faux sweetness from a distance of six feet, "go back into your room and spray this stuff on everything you own. We'll send someone to check on you in a bit. Take care now, and above all else always remember, Mommy loves."

"Please dear Lord," I prayed under my breath, "don't let the other kids get it. The weekend is quickly approaching and I know You know how awful it is to be house bound with all of them."

I started making prayers of promises right then and there. "I vow to volunteer more, tolerate slow drivers, and oh dear God in heaven, if you spare me this hateful flu, I promise to be kind to that chipper checker at Wal-Mart for the rest of my natural life." And finally—when I was certain that the Mother Of The Month people weren't listening—I added for effect, "Give it to the children if you must, but spare me."

Just as I feared, children number two and three were hit with it the next day. But number two was easily coerced into thinking he was feeling fine after a round of medication, and number three simply complained of an inability to breathe through his right nostril. Still fearing I'd catch it myself, I stocked up on anti-toxins, pushed fluids, and doused the house with disinfectant spray.

I'm fairly certain the Good Lord must have viewed me as nothing short of selfish, because I got it all right, and full bore. Never before had a flu hit me so hard. My throat swelled shut and my eyes felt like sandpaper. I kept going as long as I could, but somewhere between peanut brittle and mistletoe, I finally gave in. Armed with a blanket, a box of Kleenex, and a good decorating magazine, I headed to my room.

I had barely closed my eyes when a child arrived at my side and announced, "It's time to go."

"You are right," I replied, barely above a whisper. "Tell the priest if he wants to administer last rites, I'd like to do it before *Days of Our Lives* comes on."

Completely ignoring me, he said, "Hurry up, Mom. All of the other kids are waiting."

Fearing the worst, I quickly asked, "Are we hosting a party?"

"No, but you're in charge of car pooling, and the team's counting on you to get us to the game on time.

"But my throat is thick and I can barely swallow."

"I know," he replied with as much sympathy as a child of his age could muster, "you totally look like garbage. Here, I've brought your sweater and some running shoes."

"But you don't understand," I protested as he pulled me out of bed, "I think I'm going to that big winter wonderland in the sky."

"Great, you can drop us off at practice on the way."

I'm not dousing anything around here with disinfectant spray ever again. In fact, I'm going to breathe directly on the very next person who walks through that door.

84

CAP'N TIGHTWAD PUTS LID ON SPENDING

Sometimes I think my beloved spouse would have fared better if he'd chosen to live out a meager existence as a lonely old miser. He could have spent his golden years staring at his stacks of coins and rooms full of money. When the harsh winter winds blew, he could have balanced his checkbook to his heart's content without ever wondering why a good deal of money went to a place called The Pottery Barn.

Instead, he met and married a woman who not only purchased green beans in bulk, but also thought a portfolio was an expensive notebook from the kids' school supply list.

It's a wonder we've made it through so many years of marriage unscathed. While I tend to think that $9.99 per month is a cheap investment for extended cell phone minutes, he begs to differ. "Take that times twelve," he says in response. "That $9.99 doesn't sound so cheap at $119.88 per year, now does it?"

Well no, nothing sounds cheap when you take it times 12. He even used that line to shoot down my dream for a state of the art blender at several easy payments of $6.99.

To make financial dilemmas even worse, that darn Santa was mighty good to the kids this past Christmas season. He brought Nike sweatshirts, DVD players, and—when the time was right—he purchased name brand basketball shoes that make kids happy where ere they go.

Then—with a twinkle of his eye and a twitch of his nose—Santa left us with a "ho ho ho," and one big fat Master Card bill to go. Imagine my beloved's chagrin when that happy little bill showed up in the mail.

"Look at the enormity of this thing!" he exclaimed as he broke into a sweat. "How much did you pay for fruitcakes and eggnog and what is the cost for this stinking gadget?" he asked with a frown.

"It's not a gadget. It's a technological miracle."

"What the heck does it do?"

I tried to think up something clever, but I honest to gosh have no clue as to what the Ipod does. Therefore I simply responded with, "It makes our kid look cool."

Along with the credit card bills came the high utility bills, the bill from the butcher, and hey, that cup of cheer wasn't simply going to pay for itself.

Then came the end of the year insurance bills complete with steep premiums enveloped with pictures of happy families who sit around their Yuletide campfire as they take a moment to think about what a good neighbor their agent is.

The whole thing left the checkbook feeling empty and caused the walls of our bank accounts to bellow with a cavernous echo. Since then, Cap'n Tightwad has limited my disbursements and put a king-sized lid on spending.

"How much did you pay for this economy sized ketchup?" he asked me when I came home from the grocery store the other day. He then quickly followed that inquisition with a "Whoa! Hold on just a dag-goned minute," and "These had to be expensive!" and the ever-loving, "We can't afford small containers of potato chips that are made by people I've never heard of."

"They're called Pringles," I said as I snatched the can from him. "We've been buying them for years."

"Well, it's time to cut back on Pringles and all of the other unnecessary items."

"I suppose you want the children to give up their Cap'n Crunch?"

"Well, I certainly don't think you need this expensive can of coffee."

It was then I broke into a sweat. My knees went weak. I started to shake and my heart began to beat at a rapid pace. I could barely speak a word, but finally found the strength to defend myself with a faint breath, "You're not going to mess with my coffee."

"You don't need that expensive brand. There's nothing wrong with Folgers."

"No, there's nothing wrong with Folgers, but is there anything wrong with a woman enjoying a cup of Italian roast now and then?"

When he came into the kitchen the next morning, the room was filled with a fresh Italian aroma as I happily enjoyed my piping hot cup of a lovely roasted brew.

"I thought we decided to cut back on expenses," he was quick to point out.

"We did."

"So, where did you get the money for the coffee?"

"I found five quarters in the sweeper bag yesterday," I said with a smile. "Take that times twelve."

85

CLOSE CALL
PUTS NEW SPIN ON CALLS

Ever since a burglar attempted to break into our humble abode a couple of weeks ago, I've been down right jumpy.

Take the other day, for instance. I was in the midst of paperwork and on my fourth cup of coffee, when the phone rang. I looked at the caller ID and saw the call was coming from a cell phone. "Yeah man," the caller asked in a low and rough voice, "is Freddie there?"

Well, as you may or may not know, we've got no Freddies around here. We've got your Vernons, your Hueys, your Lawrences, and of course your Little Charlies. On a cold day when the kids are home and everyone is stuck inside, we've got your Idiots and Stupid Morons, but never—not once throughout the history of the family—have we had a Freddie. I told the man, "You have the wrong number."

He didn't say "goodbye", as a normal caller would have—rather, he sat there breathing. So I did as any sane person who was on her fourth cup of coffee would have done and I hung up on him.

Normally, I would have gone back to my paperwork and dismissed the call as a simple wrong number. But I guess I decided it'd be more fun to freak out. I heard a voice in my head that reminded me of a persistent kid—"Are the doors locked?" the voice asked. "Are they really locked? Can you be absolutely certain? Oh, sure, we checked them this morning and a couple of times before lunch and then checked them all again when we thought we heard a sound, but are we *sure* they're locked?"

I knew I was being paranoid. But I couldn't help wondering if it was God, Himself, telling me, "They're coming to take you away, ha, ha. They're coming to take you away."

Hey, it happens.

I thought perhaps I was suffering Post Traumatic Stress Syndrome or perhaps some new affliction entitled, "Some Guy Simply Takes a Screw Driver to the Door and Now You're Always Freaking Out." Either way I grabbed my coffee went to make sure all of the doors were locked—again.

En route, I heard my cell phone beeping with a missed call—and you know how something like a beeping cell phone can be in the movies? Well, my imagination is nothing, if not overactive, and loves to play "Spooky Movie" in my head. Therefore, my brain decided it'd be fun to take me to the cell phone in four jerking motions and I could hear a pound of the drums with each one. *Boom-boom, Boom-boom, Boom-boom.*

Or it could have just been the beating of my heart.

When I finally reached the cell phone, I noticed that I missed two calls at or about the same time the man with the low and rough voice had phoned and I began shaking like a leaf. I looked to see who had called, and who do you think it was who had rung me twice? Was it my mother calling to say she'd like to take the kids for the weekend? Was it eldest son calling to say he'd like to spend an evening at home? Could it have been my husband calling for a mid-day, "I just called to say I love you—I just called to say how much I care?"

Oh, heck no!

The calls came from the same number the man with the low and rough voice had called from when he phoned to see if Freddie was here.

And we don't have a Freddie!

So I wasn't happy. After all, who makes a wrong phone number to both someone's home and their cell phone? And who has a Freddie just hanging about in the middle of the day?

The suspense can really build at a time like this. And if I were a burglar-mystery writer, I'd go on to say how I went outside because that's what stupid people in burglar-mysteries do. And I'd say that when I was the most frightened and the barometric pressure had changed with the fear of the moment, a cat jumped in my path and scared the bejiggers out of me and I breathed in a sigh of relief right before a gloved hand covered my mouth.

But it wasn't a burglar-mystery, it was a real moment in the life of a woman with a caffeine-induced imagination that likes to play "Spooky Movie." And it wasn't a burglar calling to verify my location—it was a business acquaintance who had all of my phone numbers who was simply trying to call Freddie.

I still don't know who Freddie is, but I'll tell you this, I am so switching to decaf.

86

WHO COULD HAVE THROWN COOKIE AWAY?

The outside of my refrigerator hasn't been free of clutter since the first day we sent our darling to preschool. I remember it as if it were only yesterday. I can still see him with his freshly combed hair, his little backpack, and his new sneakers that could make him jump higher than Michael Jordan.

When I picked him up later that afternoon, he came out the door wearing a smile and toting the largest piece of paper I had ever seen. In fact, the paper was of such astronomic proportions I could have—if I so desired—covered the West wall of the house with it. It was plastered with cotton balls, smeared with wet paint, and sported a plethora of glitter and glue. "What have we here?" I asked with a grimace.

"It's a picture of the world," he replied with a grin. "Ms. Bliss helped me make it—and she said we should put it someplace safe until it dries."

"And how long does Ms. Bliss assume the drying will take?" I asked as the wind came up and tried to carry my child and his artwork away like a kite.

"Ms. Bliss said I should put it up for a couple of days and that we should be very careful not to wrinkle it on the way home. Can we put the baby somewhere else?"

As it turns out, the over-sized artwork wasn't an isolated incident but a trend there at the preschool—something they were known for. In fact, each and every time young Vernon exited the building, he was toting projects large enough to paper the walls, the driveway, and the upper half of the Eastern Hemisphere.

It's not that I didn't appreciate Vernon's artistic talents or cherish each elegant piece he brought into our home. I simply had no place to display 7,438 square feet of imagination.

Yet, Vernon was so proud. "Grandma," he exclaimed to my mother when she came to visit, "you'll never guess what we made at school today."

Grandma has been known to enjoy my misery, so it didn't surprise me when she stifled her laughs and answered him with faux sincerity, "What did you make today, Darling? Wait a minute. Let Grandma guess. Could it be a picture of the Northern Horizon up to and including the Rocky Mountains?"

"No, Silly," Vernon responded. "We made a life-sized replica of Pocatello, Idaho, out of macaroni. I hand glued each noodle so my Mom can hang it on the wall in the formal dining room."

To add insult to injury, Ms. Bliss never sent home seasonal artwork in time to display it for the corresponding holidays. Therefore, we exhibited king-sized pilgrims at Christmas, proudly presented a six-foot Santa on the fridge for Valentines Day, and—just to shake things up a bit—we had a lovely Easter egg collage destroyed by the fireworks on the fourth of July.

It was late in the summer following my child's stint at the Oversized Art Preschool when I gave in to defeat and admitted to myself that we couldn't proudly hang each and every item that the young man had ever put a crayon to.

I'd saved his chunky China collage, his astronomic replica of the Atlantic, and an oversized scribble of a smiling blob in an "A" line dress with "Mommy" scrawled beneath it. It was time to throw some things away.

But it wasn't easy. I waited until the time was right and I was alone. Being careful not to make a sound and cautiously looking all around me, I crept into the kitchen. I pulled the neodymium magnet that was holding his king-sized replica of the Cookie Monster onto the side of the fridge and then carefully carried the oversized artwork to the garage.

I crept back into the house covered with sweat and raw fear hoping against all hope that my shrewdness would go undiscovered. Although I was riddled with guilt, a small part of me felt liberated and free.

"You won't even believe it," I heard a voice exclaim from the garage only moments later. "Someone put Cookie in the dumpster!"

I stood in the corner and tried to feign surprise, but I must have had guilt written all over my face. Because as my little darling brushed coffee grounds off one of Cookie's eyeballs, he turned and looked at me with pain and disappointment. "Was it you, Mommy? Did you throw Cookie in the trash?"

"What's that smell?" my husband of many years asked as he walked in the door later that afternoon.

"Vernon found one of his king-sized works of art in a pizza box under last night's bean surprise," one of the kids answered. The whole family turned and looked at me as Pat asked—as if he were dumbfounded—"Who would have thrown that away?"

And that, my dear friends, is the closest I've come to a clean refrigerator in years.

87

NO TOMFOOLERY AND I MEAN IT!

Parents use many creative ways to discipline their little dears. There are the spankers, the time-outers, and the soft spoken damsels who like to lean over and ask the little guy who just pulled down the nick-knack shelf, "What better choices could we have made here, Johnny?"

I have found that I always suffer more than the kids with any form of punishment I hand out. It's like the old adage says, "This is going to hurt me a lot more than it's going to hurt you."

If things worked like I wanted them to, I'd be able to eliminate arguments over bathroom rights, front seat battles, and the ever-loving dinner table brawl, with a firm look and one simple, "and I mean it."

But my children don't take me seriously unless I scream. I have to shout from the rooftops, make the trusses rumble, and—if I chastise effectively—I can be heard as far away as Montana.

Not that I like to scream, mind you. Even though I do mean it when I say I mean it, the kids don't really think I mean it unless I'm screaming and it gives me a sore throat.

See how I suffer?

I was keeping all of this in mind the other night when we had planned to have guests over to dinner. With good and decent people in attendance at our home, I knew screaming would not be an option and time-outs would not only be a good way to keep my brood under control, they might also be pain free for me.

I gathered my boys around me. "We're having company tonight so you all need to be on your best behavior. We'll need no commentary from the bathroom, we don't need to rehash your brother's flu, and above all else, there's to be no tomfoolery."

The kids hate it when I limit their tomfoolery.

I lectured in a stern and determined manner. I gave orders, outlined consequences, and told the children, "Under no circumstances is this family to come to blows. We need to make these people think that you are disciplined." Then I added with a touch of firmness, "and I mean it."

Things went well for the first course or two. The children visited nicely, kept hands to themselves and one of the boys even complimented my pasta. Then the little dears finished their meals, cleared their plates, and—just like the little angels they can be—they vacated the area.

I was so proud.

The adult conversation was somewhere between the high cost of energy and the probability black currants may thwart memory loss, when the first blood-curdling scream could be heard coming from the basement. A weaker mother would have dropped her noodle then and there and broke into a dead run.

But I, as a seasoned parent, simply blew on my spaghetti and took another bite. I suppose I thought if I could pretend the scream hadn't occurred, others could be convinced. But it was only seconds before the next scream took place, making it evident to all that the fight had escalated.

"I'm sure they're just reenacting something they've seen on PBS," I said with a forced smile and then I excused myself and left the room.

"You boys are not being nice," I whispered to the little whippersnappers as I showed them to their corners. "Now, I want you to sit here and not make a peep." Then I pointed at the big clock on the shelf, told them they each got 10 minutes to think about their actions, and I walked away. I took a moment to calm my nerves, smooth my disposition, and then I returned to the dinner party as if I'd simply stepped out to spritz my hair.

Several minutes passed and the conversation in the kitchen had come to a lull. When the men began to discuss sports, my mind started to wander. I thought about grocery lists, stock options, and whether or not my new nail hardener was doing the trick. Just then, one of my little darlings bellowed from his corner, "Six minutes of time out left to go!" Then he paused for effect before he added, "and all is well!"

Moments later another kid updated his brother's announcement with, "Five minutes left to go," and again followed it with the proverbial, "and all's well!"

The guests turned to look at me and naturally, they all snickered. It wasn't until I walked around the corner and hollered, "Now that's enough!" that the kids piped down.

It would have been nice if I could have said it without hollering it, but I hadn't and the damage was done. I'm a screamer and now that the word was out, I roared loud enough to rattle the trusses with an angry, "and I mean it!"

I suffer so.

88

DEATH BY MIRRORS AT THE CLOTHING STORE

You know, I really hate my clothes. I've tried to bargain with my closet and make peace with my trousers, but I've grown to despise every garment I own. No matter what the season or the day, regardless of the occasion or the temperature, I've found that I don't have a dang thing to wear.

For reasons we may never understand, I still have that darn Madonna collection from the 80s. My stretch pant collection simply has to go and it's time I realize hanging onto the size-6 assortment will never become an inspiration to cut my dress size in half—I don't care how cheap that tiny belt was.

I've got leg warmers in all of the wrong colors, theme sweaters with no topic, and skirts I would never wear in a million years. However, they would look great on someone with small hips, so I'm forced to hang onto them out of spite.

My closet is voluminous. It's full, and when I opened the door just last Tuesday, I realized it belongs to a woman half my size with little or no taste. So, I did as women in my situation are prone to do—I styled my hair, applied fresh lipstick, and strolled to the car sporting a smile and a department store credit card.

I hit a sale rack with corduroys for $14.99, faded jeans for a fraction of the original cost, and dress slacks that were going for a price I could not afford to turn my back on. Feeling victorious, I went to try on the clothes. I was eager to become the fashionable person I was always meant to be.

Once I was in the dressing room, I piled my stack of clothing on a small bench, hung my purse on a hook, and set about selecting my first garment. It was then I discovered the dressing room had been designed by a thin person with a mean streak. Who else would have thought it would be great to equip such a room with three large mirrors? And if the kaleidoscope view of one's body weren't enough to send one screaming to the nearest diet center, the mirror on the fourth wall that was large enough to reflect the hind end of Shamoo would certainly do it.

What kind of nut, I ask you, wants to see every part of her body without so much as turning her head? Who wants to know what people see as we walk away? While the concept of a full body view might appeal to 19-year-old runway models, it's certainly not exactly my idea of a stroll in the park.

The mirrors in my home have been hand selected. They all bend in the middle just right and protect the fragile image I see in my mind's eye when I think of myself. In fact, every reflective object in my house has been delicately placed so I look to be about 6' tall and thin as a rail with a mid-section reminiscent of Cindy Crawford's.

The designer of the dressing room there at the department store seemed determined to shatter that image. Still, I decided I could try on the clothes and not look at myself. I would get the clothes off and on and get the heck out of the dressing room before the figure being reflected in the mirror burnt an image on my retinas that would destroy my self-image forever.

I'd barely placed a toe into the first leg of the corduroys, when I couldn't help but steal a glance. It was like a train wreck—you just can't help but look even though you know you're going to be horrified.

The room was like a brightly-lit kaleidoscope of cellulite. Suddenly, I didn't even know how I was ever able to leave the house in this body—especially knowing that unless I move about disguised as a billboard, someone is bound to notice my mis-proportioned hips.

I slipped back into my fat pants, picked up my purse, and ran out of the dressing room before I gave in to temptation and—like a fool—decided to take another look. I marched back through the department store, past the cheap corduroys and faded jeans for half price, and headed back home to give my closet another look.

And you know what? With a baggy shirt, and the right lighting, those stretch pants didn't look too bad.

89

CURSE WORDS AND CONFESSION

I think it's absolutely appalling when parents say bad words to their children and I feel bad every time I do it.

The truth is, my little dears can be exhilaration, animation and total frustration all wrapped up into one enchilada. Aunt Mary best described a mother's feelings for her children when she said, "You wouldn't take a million dollars for them, but you wouldn't pay a dime for another batch just like them."

Take an incident that occurred last week, for instance. As I busied myself by matching socks in the laundry room, the children prepared afternoon snacks in the kitchen. One of my children had taken his favorite bowl out of the cupboard and prepared to pour himself a bowl of cereal. Just then Huey, my "would-be-a-priest child," decided he should have his brother's favorite bowl instead. Huey did as older brothers do best in this kind of situation—he flexed his juvenile muscles and ripped the bowl out of his brother's hands with brute force.

The younger brother, of course, responded as younger ones always do—by screaming loudly and vigorously at the top of his cotton-pickin' lungs, "I'm tellin' Mom."

I just hate it when the kids tell Mom.

"For heaven's sake Huey!" I hollered from the laundry room, "give him back the stinking bowl!"

Huey gave the bowl back to Little Charlie but not before he gave him a quick bonk on the head and fight No. 2 commenced with all the shouting and violence of a Martin Scorsese movie.

I hollered again from the laundry room and gently asked the children to calm down and with the wisdom of Solomon I even offered to cut the bowl in half.

But it was only a matter of time before I heard them start to hit, smack, and jab.

I became angrier by the second. I took deep breaths and wished for either an out-of-body experience or a Calgon bath to take me away. I mean, after all, isn't it a mother's right to match socks in peace?

"Huey," I finally screamed above the noise and hostilities, "just get your own" (and this is where I failed as a mother) "*&#% bowl!"

Silence fell over the abode. The clocks stopped ticking. The earth stopped spinning. The air was still—and I'm quite certain the barometric pressure in the kitchen rose a notch.

"OOOOOOOOOH!" I heard my oldest child whisper, "you just made Mom cuss."

"So," I heard Huey respond, "I've heard her cuss before."

"Not unless she's real mad," said another child.

"Well then," Huey replied, "she must be mad a lot."

I walk through the valley of the shadow of death to bring children into this world and what do I get in return? Judgment.

Later that week, I loaded all of the kids up and took them to church for confession. I got on my knees and took time for reflection and came up with some good sins to disclose. Feeling satisfied and comfortable with my soul searching, I sat on the bench and waited for my turn to talk to the priest.

It was then I noticed young Huey staring at me intently. "What?" I whispered to him.

He looked at me for a minute and then shook his head and responded with, "Nothing."

"Well, why are you staring at me like that?"

"I was just wondering."

"Wondering what?"

"What you're going to confess."

Feeling frustrated, I replied, "That's between me and God."

"Just tell me," he persisted. "What are you going to confess?"

"I'll tell ya what, you become a priest and then I'll tell you what my sins are."

"Well," he whispered, as he scooted closer, "I heard you gossiping to Grandma last week. Is that a sin?"

"No, that's not a sin," I retorted to the little snip as I mentally added gossip to my list of transgressions. "Now mind your own business."

He was quiet again, but only for a minute. He looked around the church and fidgeted with his hands. Then he put his arm around my shoulder and with his face an inch away from mine he said, "Well, you cuss sometimes, you might want to mention that."

You know Aunt Mary is right. I wouldn't trade that child for a lifetime supply of spending money. But I wouldn't give a plug nickel for another one just like him.

90

A NEW EMPTY NESTER SHOWS NO MERCY

My good friend Karen is about to become an empty nester. She's anticipating TV time, empty laundry baskets, and—if what she says is really true—her days of compositions and sentence structure are coming to an end. Meanwhile, I'm still choking on solar systems and adverbs.

Karen's buying dinners for two while I stock up on Spaghetti-O's. She's looking at sports cars while I'm changing the tires on the Suburban. She's keeping track of her last ticket taking events, science projects—and actually has the nerve to brag about it.

Although I saw her at parent/teacher conferences just last week, I didn't pay her much mind. I was way too busy being the model parent. I listened with interest to Mr. Weber's assessment of my child's academics. I promised the music teacher that I'd let the kids bang on our piano at home. And when I discussed the muscular-skeletal system with our Health-man, Mr. Dodson, I told him that my son's aspirations to land himself smack dab in the winner's circle on Jeopardy could be achieved now that he had a full and complete knowledge of metatarsals.

In fact, it wasn't until I sat across from the math teacher, Mrs. Murphy, I started to feel inadequate. Although she started out simple, it wasn't long before she lost me with formulas and equations. Then she began to explain how wonderfully the class had learned to solve quadratic equations by graphing, factoring, completing the square, and finding the square footage for a parabola.

Is it me, or does a parabola sound like an Italian dish? To be honest, I was starting to get one of those headaches that hit you right between the eyes when I noticed Karen floating by. Not just walking—mind you—but actually floating.

As other parents listened and heeded the words and observations of the faculty with tears and frowns, Karen moved about the group with a smile. She went from teacher to teacher, listening here, chuckling there, and often times shaking hands with the faculty as she departed.

At one point in time, she actually approached the principal—a man I've been trying to avoid since the winter of 1996.

"Girl," I whispered as I sidled up alongside her, "have you been hitting the sauce?"

"Gosh no!" she responded in a dreamy tone, "why would you ask?"

"Because you're smiling," I answered as I looked around. "Who smiles at parent/teacher conferences?"

"Oh, this is better than a 95 percent off sale," she responded. "This is better than, close-out specials, and the perfect sugar-free chocolate. You see, my dear and unfortunate friend, this is my last parent/teacher's conference." And then she leaned in real close, opened her eyes real wide, and smiled even bigger before she added, "FOREVER!"

As if that weren't enough, she called me later that day to really rub things in. When I answered the phone, I could hear an adding machine running in the background.

Apparently she wasn't about to let it go.

"I noticed you became interested in some numbers today during your conference with Mrs. Murphy," she said in her best sing/song voice. "So I thought I would draw on my experience and work up some numbers on my own. Now, in reviewing my spreadsheets and going over my calculations, you, my dear friend, have—let's see, carry the nine, divided by 312, oh my! You have approximately 6,423 parent/teacher's conferences to go.

"I also took the liberty to take it one step further and calculate math assignments and if one begins doubling the averages and adding statistics in there, you are looking at—let me see, 12 x 12 (46) to the square root of 3 - 18 > 4* x 8}m 3 to the 4th power of 9, 8 pie over [5] to the 9th power....WOW! Those are certainly some big numbers. As for me—well, my favorite number is 0. That's right, 0 parent-teacher conferences, 0 math assignments, and how many algebraic equations are in my future? Carry the four and hit total....oh, that's right, ZERO!"

If Karen's figures are correct, I may not have a free moment until June of 2037. While Karen is loafing on her lounge chair and organizing committees for her card playing groups, I'll be catering to basketball players and trying to help my child find the square root of 6,029.

She can boast if she wants to, but by this time next year, Karen will wish she were me. I know it's true. It won't be long until the sound of her empty nest sends her running to my house and begging to do some homework.

But, I've no time to dwell on that. I'm awfully busy. We've got three tests, two projects, and—as an extra treat—I thought I'd whip up a special batch of parabolas for the children's dinner tonight.

Another Review at MyShelf.com

Are We There Yet?
By Lori Clinch

Reviewer: Lynda E. Lukow
Copyright: ©MyShelf.com

Reading *Are We There Yet* is like drinking a cup of chamomile tea while lying on a down mattress - soothing comfort feathered with ticklish humor.

Lori Clinch is the quintessential woman. When not writing her weekly column for a Nebraskan newspaper, she's juggling a jam-packed life. Her parents still book her guilt trips. Her husband occasionally acts like a child. Her sisters-in-law clip coupons and shop with a vengeance. Her quirky friends add spice (and competition) to her life.

However, her primary focus is raising four sons. She dreads the last day of school and celebrates the end of summer recess. Homework, chores, Christmas lists, driving lessons, and sibling rivalry - each snippet is packed with witty candor. Whether her boys hide her scissors or bring home dead snakes, she manages to find absurdity in every child-rearing adventure.

Many authors have attempted to fill Erma Bombeck's slippers, but none have come as close as Lori Clinch. Her universal topics will strike chords in most parents. Her straightforward style and playful wit makes pleasant reading after a long day. Got a family-induced stress headache? Forget the Tylenol! Grab *Are We There Yet* instead!

The author sincerely thanks the owners of MyShelf.com for this review and for their permission to reprint this review.

WHEN I HAVE KIDS
by Dixie Eckhoff

"When I have kids," she told us all,
"they will not misbehave.
They'll show some class and follow
on the road that I shall pave.

"My kids will be obedient
and listen when I speak.
They'll pick their toys up daily,
clean their own rooms twice a week.

"They'll never, never lie to me,
of this you can be sure.
My kids will want to please me.
They'll be innocent and pure.

"I don't believe in fighting
like I've seen your children do.
Sometimes your children act as though
they should be in a zoo.

"My children, on the other hand,
will never disagree.
They'll always see things my way.
They would never challenge me."

I cocked my head, suppressed a smile,
and said, "You are amazing.
I simply cannot wait to meet
these children you'll be raising.

"I'm glad you have the answers,
to accomplish all your deeds.
They'll never get to blame you,
for neglecting all their needs.

"So, when you have achieved your goal,
and all that you surmise,
I'd like to shake your hand
when you receive the Nobel Prize!"

Dixie Eckhoff is the author of a delightful book of humorous stories and poems titled, Just a Little Bull...and a few cow tales, published by The Old 101 Press. Her poetry has been published in several periodicals and has won both state and national awards! Thank you, Dixie, for allowing me to use this special poem!

Don't Make Me Pull Over!
by Lori Clinch

Lori Clinch was born and raised in North Platte, Nebraska, a hotbed of material for writers whose passion it is to make people laugh. Her parents approached difficulties with a sense of humor and Lori learned from them early that it's a great way to cope with life. A friend of Lori's — the one who once decorated her mantle with poison ivy — says Lori's special talent is to take everyday situations and help people see the humor in them.

Lori and her husband, Pat, have four boys, all of whom provide fine fodder for her writing.

Lori is a columnist for The North Platte Telegraph. She was voted favorite columnist of the year in both 2004 and 2005. Her column is now syndicated in 13 newspapers in New Jersey, too, and reaches more than 260,000 readers every week. The best is yet to come!

From THE OLD 101 PRESS:

"They say you can't take it with you, but you can. When you die all the stories in your head go, too."

Billie Thornburg, founder of The Old Hundred And One Press, and author of *Bertie and Me*, *Bertie and Me and Miles Too*, and *Sandhills Kid In The City*, is dedicated to encouraging people to write the stories of their lives. At age ninety, Billie wrote her first book and started The Old Hundred And One Press to publish history as told by those who've lived it.

Today, Billie is 94 years of age and believes she has a new lease on life. She completed her fourth book in late 2005. *City and Prairie Bones* is a compilation of stories of life in North Platte during the years when it earned its reputation as "Little Chicago." Billie is hard at work on her fifth book which she plans to title, *Angels on Horseback*, and which she confesses, "may not be my last book."

Readers can reach Billie at:

The Old Hundred and One Press
2220 Leota Avenue
North Platte, NE 69101

www.theold101press.com
Phone: (308) 532-1748

NOW AVAILABLE

Bertie and Me...kids on a ranch
by *Billie Lee Snyder-Thornburg*
Billie Snyder Thornburg's first book. A humorous and historical account of two little girls growing up on a Nebraska Sandhills ranch in the early 1900's.

ISBN: 0-9721613-0-9
Pages: 160   **Publish Date:** October 1, 2002
Publisher: The Old 101 Press Publishing
For All Ages **Price:** Only $18.95 - Paperback

Bertie and Me and Miles Too
by *Billie Lee Snyder-Thornburg*
Billie Snyder Thornburg continues telling of early Sandhills life with stories of her brother, Miles, home remedies, Model T's. privies, and old time roundups.

ISBN: 0-9721613-3-3
Pages: 144   **Publish Date:** December 1, 2003
Publisher: The Old 101 Press Publishing
For All Ages **Price:** Only $16.95 - Paperback

Sandhills Kid in the City
by *Billie Lee Snyder Thornburg*
Ride along with "...Bertie and me who were still trying to find our places in the big world around us" as they move from their beloved Sandhills ranch to Oregon to attend high school. Rich, exciting adventures!

ISBN: 0-9721613-7-6
Pages: 144   **Publish Date:** June 1, 2004
Publisher: The Old Hundred and One Press

City & Prairie Bones
by *Billie Snyder Thornburg*
Billie Snyder Thornburg's fourth book takes a look at life in the vicinity of North Platte, Nebraska. Billie focuses, especially on the period during which North Platte came to be known as "Little Chicago".

ISBN: 0-9721613-5-X
Pages: 152   **Publish Date:** November 2005
Publisher: The Old Hundred and One Press
For Young Adult & Adult **Price:** Only $14.95 - Paperback

If Morning Never Comes
by Bill VandenBush
The powerful story of a soldier's near-death experience in Vietnam. "A priceless gift to anyone in search of their own spiritual path...enormously inspirational" - Nora Fitzgerald

ISBN: 0-9721613-4-1
Pages: 232   **Publish Date:** December 1, 2003
Publisher: The Old 101 Press Publishing
For All Ages   **Price:** Only $14.95 - Paperback

Miracle of the Ozarks
by Chester Funkhouser
The touching story of a grandfather's love, a child's belief in miracles, and survival of the human heart in the face of cancer, war wounds, and loss. The reader will fall in love with the beauty and spirit of the Ozarks.

ISBN: 0-9721613-8-4
Pages: 160   **Publish Date:** 2004
Publisher: The Old Hundred and One Press
For All Ages   **Price:** Only $14.95 - Paperback

Are We There Yet?
by Lori Clinch
A hilarious look at one woman's experiences raising four sons. Not meant as a parenting guide, but definitely encouraging to parents who need to know someone else has kids like theirs.

ISBN: 0-9721613-9-2
Pages: 300   **Publish Date:** May 1, 2004
Publisher: The Old Hundred and One Press
For All Ages   **Price:** Only $15.95 - Paperback

Don't Make Me Pull Over!
by Lori Clinch
Many authors have attempted to fill Erma Bombeck's slippers, but none have come as close as Lori Clinch. Her universal topics will strike chords in most parents. Her straightforward style and playful wit makes pleasant reading after a long day. ~ *MyShelf.com*

ISBN: 0-9763676-4-5
Pages: 285   **Publish Date:** October 8, 2006
Publisher: The Old Hundred and One Press
For All Ages   **Price:** Only $15.95 - Paperback

Listen With The Heart
Everyday Lives Lived in the Extraordinary
by Barbara Ann Dush
Heroes are all around us if we learn to Listen With The Heart. The daily headlines scream bad news, crime, hardship, and suffering. However, behind many of those headline stories are people whose lives speak gently to us of courage, strength, and compassion if we only learn to Listen With the Heart.

ISBN: 0-9721613-1-7
Pages: 160   **Publish Date:** March 12, 2005
Publisher: The Old Hundred and One Press
For All Ages   **Price:** Only $15.95 - Paperback

Just A Little Bull . . . and a few cow tales
by Dixie D. Eckhoff
A collection of humorous Western poetry and a few cow tales. The zany rhymes resonate with the experience of many who grew up and/or live in rural America. You must have a strong constitution to survive your laughter when you read Dixie's book.

ISBN: 0-9721613-2-5
Pages: 136   **Publish Date:** August 8, 2005
Publisher: The Old Hundred and One Press
For All Ages   **Price:** Only $15.95 - Paperback

Well Fry Me For An Oyster!
by Dave Simpson
Dave Simpson has shared his down to earth outlook on the everyday quirks of life – both personal and social – for 32 years. Here he collects his favorite columns for your enjoyment.

ISBN: 0-9763676-1-0
Pages: 225   **Publish Date:** June 14, 2005
Publisher: The Old Hundred and One Press

ORDER FORM

Please send me _____ copies of *Bertie and Me* @ $18.95

Please send me _____ copies of *Bertie and Me and Miles Too* @ $16.95

Please send me _____ copies of *Sandhills Kid in the City* @ $16.95

Please send me _____ copies of *City and Prairie Bones* @ $14.95

Please send me _____ copies of *If Morning Never Comes* @ $14.95

Please send me _____ copies of *Are We There Yet?* @ $15.95

Please send me _____ copies of *Don't Make Me Pull Over!* @ $15.95

Please send me _____ copies of *Miracle of the Ozarks* @ $14.95

Please send me _____ copies of *Listen With The Heart* @ $15.95

Please send me _____ copies of *Just A Little Bull* @ $15.95

Please send me _____ copies of *Well Fry Me For An Oyster!* @ $15.95

TOTAL COST OF BOOKS: $ _____

NEBRASKA RESIDENTS 7% TAX: $ _____

Add $4.00 for Shipping and Handling: $ ___4.00_____

TOTAL ENCLOSED: $ _____

Name: _____

Address: _____

City, State, Zip_____

Visit our Website: www.theold101press.com

Telephone Orders: (308) 532-1748

E-Mail Orders: billielee@inebraska.com

Postal Orders: The Old Hundred and One Press
                2220 Leota
                North Platte, NE 69101